Learning Azure Functions

Build scalable cloud systems with serverless architecture

Manisha Yadav
Mitesh Soni

BIRMINGHAM - MUMBAI

Learning Azure Functions

First published: September 2017

Production reference: 1260917

Published by Packt Publishing Ltd.
Livery Place
35 Livery Street
Birmingham
B3 2PB, UK.

ISBN 978-1-78712-293-2

www.packtpub.com

Credits

Authors
Manisha Yadav
Mitesh Soni

Reviewers
Ruben Oliva Ramos
Florian Klaffenbach

Commissioning Editor
Vijin Boricha

Acquisition Editor
Divya Poojari

Content Development Editor
Deepti Thore

Technical Editor
Sneha Hanchate

Copy Editors
Laxmi Subramanian
Safis Editing

Project Coordinator
Shweta H Birwatkar

Proofreader
Safis Editing

Indexer
Pratik Shirodkar

Graphics
Tania Dutta

Production Coordinator
Shantanu Zagade

About the Authors

Manisha Yadav is a system engineer. She has worked on Java-based projects, web application projects, and Azure and AWScloud services. She has experience of working with tools such as Jenkins and SonarQube.

She also has work experience on databases such as MYSQL and MongoDB, and frontend technology such as HTML, CSS, JavaScript, and Angular JS.

She loves to explore new cloud services and new technologies.

She loves traveling and spending time with her family. She also likes cooking.

It gives me immense pleasure to thank the people who have helped me in this Journey. Many people contributed their time and energy on my behalf to make this book what it is. I would particularly like to thank to Nitin, Sandeep, Vaishnavi, and Rupali, who have been with me and encouraged me.

I would like to thank Mitesh; without his painstaking effort, this book would have never seen the light of day.

The patience and willingness to help shown by my reviewers is greatly appreciated.

Mitesh Soni is an avid learner with 10 years of experience in the IT industry. He is an SCJP, SCWCD, VCP, IBM Urbancode, and IBM Bluemix certified professional, and Certified Scrum Master. He loves DevOps and cloud computing and he also has an interest in programming in Java. He finds design patterns fascinating. He believes a picture is worth a thousand words.

He occasionally contributes to etutorialsworld.com. He loves to play with kids, fiddle with his camera, and take photographs at Indroda Park. He is addicted to taking pictures without knowing many technical details. He lives in the capital of Mahatma Gandhi's home state.

Mitesh has authored the following books with Packt:

- *Jenkins Essentials, Second Edition*
- *DevOps Bootcamp*
- *Implementing DevOps with Microsoft Azure*
- *DevOps for Web Development*
- *Jenkins Essentials*
- *Learning Chef*

I've missed more than 9,000 shots in my career. I've lost almost 300 games. 26 times, I've been trusted to take the game-winning shot and missed. I've failed over and over and over again in my life. And that is why I succeed

— Michael Jordan4.

I've always thanked a lot of people who have been instrumental in contributing to my life's journey until now, but I guess it's time to really acknowledge that one person who has been with me as long as I can remember.

With this book, I would like to thank the one and only invisible, yet omnipresent Almighty. We share a mutual love-and-hate relationship and I really value it. You were always there equally during my good and bad times and without You, I wouldn't have made it this far!

Special thanks to Manisha for helping me in this journey; without her this book was not possible.

Last but not least, I want to thank all who taught me how to love myself, first!

About the Reviewers

Ruben Oliva Ramos is a computer systems engineer from Tecnologico of León Institute, with a master's degree in computer and electronic systems engineering, teleinformatics and networking specialization from University of Salle Bajio in Leon, Guanajuato Mexico. He has more than 5 years of experience in developing web applications to control and monitor devices connected with Arduino and Raspberry Pi using web frameworks and cloud services to build the Internet of Things applications.

He is a mechatronics teacher at University of Salle Bajio and teaches students on the master's degree in design and engineering of mechatronics systems, also works at Centro de Bachillerato Tecnologico Industrial 225 in Leon, Guanajuato Mexico, teaching subjects such as electronics, robotics and control, automation, and microcontrollers on Mechatronics Technician Career, Consultant and developer projects in areas such as monitoring systems and datalogger data using technologies such as Android, iOS, Windows Phone, HTML5, PHP, CSS, Ajax, JavaScript, Angular, ASP .NET databases: SQlite, mongoDB, MySQL, WEB Servers: Node.js, IIS, hardware programming: Arduino, Raspberry pi, Ethernet Shield, GPS and GSM/GPRS, ESP8266, control and monitor Systems for data Acquisition and Programming.

He has written a book for Packt Publishing titled *Internet of Things Programming with JavaScript*. He has also written *Monitoring, Controlling, and Acquisition of Data with Arduino* and *Visual Basic .NET for Alfaomega*.

I would like to thank my savior and lord, Jesus Christ, for giving me strength and courage to pursue this project; to my dearest wife, Mayte; our two lovely sons, Ruben and Dario; to my dear father, Ruben; my dearest mom, Rosalia; my brother, Juan Tomas; and my sister, Rosalia, whom I love, for all their support while reviewing this book, for allowing me to pursue my dream and tolerating not being with them after my busy day job.

I'm very grateful to Pack Publishing for giving me the opportunity to collaborate as an author and reviewer, to belong to this honest and professional team.

Florian Klaffenbach started in 2004 with his IT career as first and second level IT support technician and IT salesman trainee for a B2B online shop. After that, he changed to a small company working as IT project manager, planning, implementing, and integrating from industrial plants and laundries into enterprise IT. After spending some years, he changed his path to Dell Germany. There he started from scratch as an enterprise technical support analyst and later worked on a project to start Dell technical communities and support over social media in Europe and outside of the U.S. Currently, he is working as technology solutions professional for Microsoft specialized on hybrid microsoft cloud infrastructure.

In addition to his job, he is active as a Microsoft blogger and lecturer. He blogs, for example, on his own page Datacenter-Flo.de or Brocade Germany Community. Together with a very good friend, he founded the Windows Server User Group, Berlin, to create network of Microsoft ITPros in Berlin. Florian is maintaining a very tight network to many vendors such as Cisco, Dell, or Microsoft and Communities. This helps him to grow his experience and to get the best out of a solution for his customers. Since 2016, he is also the co-chairman of the Azure Community, Germany. In April 2016, Microsoft awarded Florian as the Microsoft Most Valuable Professional for Cloud and Datacenter Management. In 2017, after joining Microsoft, Florian became an MVP reconnect member.

Florian worked for several companies and Microsoft partners such as Dell Germany, CGI Germany, and msg services ag. Now he has joined Microsoft Germany in a technical presales role and supports customers to get started with hybrid cloud infrastructures and topics.

He has also reviewed the following books for Packt:

- *Microsoft Azure Storage Essentials*
- *Mastering Microsoft Azure Development*

www.PacktPub.com

For support files and downloads related to your book, please visit www.PacktPub.com.

Did you know that Packt offers eBook versions of every book published, with PDF and ePub files available? You can upgrade to the eBook version at www.PacktPub.com and as a print book customer, you are entitled to a discount on the eBook copy. Get in touch with us at service@packtpub.com for more details.

At www.PacktPub.com, you can also read a collection of free technical articles, sign up for a range of free newsletters and receive exclusive discounts and offers on Packt books and eBooks.

https://www.packtpub.com/mapt

Get the most in-demand software skills with Mapt. Mapt gives you full access to all Packt books and video courses, as well as industry-leading tools to help you plan your personal development and advance your career.

Why subscribe?

- Fully searchable across every book published by Packt
- Copy and paste, print, and bookmark content
- On demand and accessible via a web browser

Customer Feedback

Thanks for purchasing this Packt book. At Packt, quality is at the heart of our editorial process. To help us improve, please leave us an honest review on this book's Amazon page at https://www.amazon.com/dp/178712293X.

If you'd like to join our team of regular reviewers, you can e-mail us at customerreviews@packtpub.com. We award our regular reviewers with free eBooks and videos in exchange for their valuable feedback. Help us be relentless in improving our products!

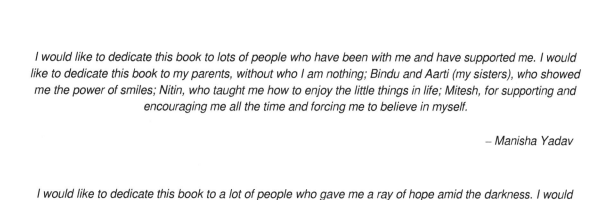

I would like to dedicate this book to lots of people who have been with me and have supported me. I would like to dedicate this book to my parents, without who I am nothing; Bindu and Aarti (my sisters), who showed me the power of smiles; Nitin, who taught me how to enjoy the little things in life; Mitesh, for supporting and encouraging me all the time and forcing me to believe in myself.

– Manisha Yadav

I would like to dedicate this book to a lot of people who gave me a ray of hope amid the darkness. I would like to dedicate this book to Shreyansh (Shreyu—my sister Jigisha's baby boy), who showed me the power of innocence and smiles; Vinay Kher, for his blessing; my parents, who are always there silently praying for me; Simba (Priyanka Agashe), for supporting and encouraging me all the time and forcing me to believe in myself; the Indian Army, and all the brave soldiers in uniform for protecting us. Please support bharatkeveer.gov.in/ *to pay homage to the brave hearts who laid down their lives in the line of duty.*

– Mitesh Soni

Table of Contents

Preface   1

Chapter 1: Introducing Microsoft Azure Services and Functions   9

    An overview of serverless architectures   10
        Cloud computing and service models   11
          Cloud computing and its basics   12
        Serverless computing   16
          Benefits   16
    Why Azure Functions?   17
    An overview of Microsoft Azure Services   24
        Regions   24
        Resource groups   26
        App Services - Microsoft Azure Web Apps   30
          App Service plan   32
        Azure Active Directory   35
        App Insights   37
    Azure Services versus AzureFunctions versus AWS Lambda   38
    Summary   39

Chapter 2: First Function App - Anatomy and Structure of a Function App   41

    Anatomy of Azure Functions   42
        Azure Function App   42
        Function code   42
        Function configuration   44
        Function settings   44
        Runtime   45
    Setting up a basic Azure Function   45
    Summary   72

Chapter 3: Application of Triggers   73

    Common types of triggers   74
    Example of creating a simple scheduled trigger   75
    HTTP trigger   81
    Event hubs   90
    Service bus   91
    Summary   92

Chapter 4: Bindings   93

Available input and output bindings   94
Types of input bindings   94
Types of output bindings   95
Types of Event Hubs   96
Event Hubs   96
    Example   96
Service Bus   103
Storage   108
Example   109
Summary   111

Chapter 5: Webhooks for Azure Functions   113

Creating a JavaScript function triggered by a Webhook   114
Using a Webhook with an Azure Function   123
Using an event with an Azure Function   126
Summary   127

Chapter 6: The Real World - Functions to Build Consumable APIs   129

Outlining a project   129
Architecting the solution   130
Building the project   131
Using storage   154
Test   155
Summary   156

Chapter 7: Managing and Deploying your Code   157

Projects in VSTS   158
Continuous Integration   167
Continuous Delivery   170
Summary   186

Chapter 8: Business Considerations   187

Monitoring of Azure Functions   188
Integration of Application Insights and Azure Functions   193
Pricing/hosting plans   201
Best practices   205
Summary   206

Chapter 9: Working with Different Languages   207

The Python Function App   208
Example   208

The PHP Function App   214

    Example   215

Summary   219

Index   221

Preface

Serverless is not actually serverless. It means that users only need to manage code/applications and not servers. The server will be managed by the service provider. We as users only pay when our code or function is executed in the serverless or in a server that is not managed by us. Scaling is based on request and pricing differs based on the service provider.

AWS Lambda and Azure Functions are two examples of serverless computing or Function as a Service. Azure Functions enable us to create serveless applications in the Microsoft Azure environment. Azure Functions are open sourced and available on GitHub. They support different languages such as C#, F#, Node.js, Python, PHP, batch, bash, or PowerShell.

It is always best to focus on building innovative applications that help businesses to grow in different dimensions. So, it is important to de-focus from provisioning, managing and maintaining servers, managing high availability, and configuring security. Azure Functions allow us to focus on building applications with a serverless architecture.

Additionally, if we can utilize DevOps practices such as Continuous Integration, Continuous Monitoring, and Continuous Delivery with approval mechanisms using Visual Studio Team Services, that is the a cherry on the cake, isn't It?

What this book covers

Chapter 1, *Introducing Microsoft Azure Services and Functions*, describes in detail the fundamental concepts and terminology to give the reader a baseline understanding of cloud computing, cloud service models, cloud deployment models, functions and some of the related concepts in Microsoft Azure.

Chapter 2, *First Function App – Anatomy and Structure of a Function App*, covers how to focus into creating our first Azure Function. We will create the Azure Function App and then we will create the Azure Function with trigger and output binding.

Chapter 3, *Application of Triggers*, provides insights on how we can create triggers. Triggers are nothing but a set of functions that get executed when some event gets fired. There are different types of triggers, such as implicit triggers, and we can also create manual triggers. In this chapter, we will cover an overview of triggers and different types of triggers such as HTTP, Event Bus, Service Bus, and Storage.

Chapter 4, *Bindings*, describes bindings in detail. In Azure Function, a binding is used to bind other Azure resources to our Azure Function. We will cover different input/output bindings in this chapter. Brief details will be given about Input bindings such as Blob storage, Storage tables, SQL tables, and NoSQL DBs. Details about output bindings such as HTTP (REST or Webhook), Blob Storage, Events, Queues and topics, Storage tables, SQL tables, NoSQL DBs, Push Notifications, and SendGrid email will also be provided. We will create an example of binding an Azure Function to the event hub, service bus and binding of Azure function with Service bus queue, and also storage.

Chapter 5, *Webhooks for Azure Functions*, covers how to create JavaScript functions triggered by Webhook, how to use Webhook with Azure Functions, and how to use an event with an Azure Function.

Chapter 6, *The Real World – Functions to Build Consumable APIs*, provides insights into how to use the previously-discussed concept of triggers. Bindings work together to bring some real-world functionality to life. First, we will give an outline of the project that we will try to implement; then, we will try to build or architect a solution. We will build the project, use storage, and then verify the whole exercise.

Chapter 7, *Managing and Deploying Your Code*, talks about DevOps practices such as Continuous Integration and Continuous Delivery using Microsoft Azure Functions and Visual Studio Team Services. DevOps is a combination of Development and Operations. DevOps is not a tool, a technology, or a framework. DevOps is a culture. It is a culture that brings improvement in the outcome and productivity of the resources. We will create a project in VSTS and then configure Continuous Integration and Continuous Delivery for Azure Functions.

Chapter 8, *Business Considerations*, covers details about how to monitor the health of Functions. Azure Functions have their own kind of monitoring, which is useful but basic. For an advanced level of monitoring, we will utilize Application Insights. Another important business consideration is to understand pricing concepts so that we can make an informed decision based on anticipated load, growth, and product roadmap. This chapter will also cover the integration of Application Insights and Azure Functions, pricing/hosting plans, and best practices.

Chapter 9, *Working with Different Languages*, shows you how to use Azure Functions with other languages such as C#, Python, F#, PHP, and JavaScript. This chapter focuses on the Python Function App and PHP Function App.

What you need for this book

This book is for beginners. This book assumes that you are familiar with at least JavaScript, Python, PHP, and other programming languages. Knowledge of these programming languages is essential considering this book to gain better insight. Having a strong understanding of program logic will provide you with the background to be productive with Azure Functions while creating serverless architecture.

As we are going to use Microsoft Azure Functions, you need to have an Azure subscription or free trail to utilize Azure Functions. For basic functions, Azure Functions can be used freely without using a Microsoft Azure Account.

In this book, we cover Continuous Integration and Continuous Delivery for Azure Functions, so it is essential to have a Visual Team Studio Services (VSTS) account and some basic knowledge of it. You can utilize the *Implementing DevOps with Microsoft Azure* book available at `https://www.amazon.com/Implementing-DevOps-Microsoft-Azure-Mitesh-ebook/dp/B01MSQWO4W` for DevOps, Microsoft Azure, and VSTS-related basic knowledge. It is good to have some knowledge of repositories such as svn and Git as in Continuous Integration and Continuous Delivery. For Azure Functions, we are going to use a VSTS repository to store the code for the functions.

Additionally, you will need access to the internet to access Azure Portal. Any normal hardware configuration is good enough, such as 4 GB RAM and 500 GB hard disk, to access Microsoft Azure Portal and work with different functions.

Who this book is for

Learning Azure Functions is for beginners. This book targets developers and system administrators who are involved in application development and are looking to automate it. Developers, technical leads, and architects too are the target readers to jumpstart Azure Functions. The reasons to jumpstart Azure Functions are to understand importance and effective usage of Serverless Architecture in application building.

Conventions

In this book, you will find a number of styles of text that distinguish between different kinds of information. Here are some examples of these styles, and an explanation of their meaning.

Code words in text, database table names, folder names, filenames, file extensions, pathnames, dummy URLs, user input, and Twitter handles are shown as follows: "We can include other contexts through the use of the `include` directive."

A block of code is set as follows:

```
{
"bindings": [
{
"name": "myBlob",
"type": "blobTrigger",
"direction": "in",
"path": "photographs/{name}",
"connection": "origphotography2017_STORAGE",
"dataType": "binary"
},
```

When we wish to draw your attention to a particular part of a code block, the relevant lines or items are set in bold:

```
"name": "myBlob",
"type": "blobTrigger",
"direction": "in",
"path": "photographs/{name}",
"connection": "origphotography2017_STORAGE",
"dataType": "binary"
},
```

Any command-line input or output is written as follows:

```
# cp /usr/src/asterisk-addons/configs/cdr_mysql.conf.sample
/etc/asterisk/cdr_mysql.conf
```

New terms and **important words** are shown in bold. Words that you see on the screen, in menus or dialog boxes for example, appear in the text like this: "clicking the **Next** button moves you to the next screen."

Warnings or important notes appear in a box like this.

 Tips and tricks appear like this.

Reader feedback

Feedback from our readers is always welcome. Let us know what you think about this book—what you liked or may have disliked. Reader feedback is important for us to develop titles that you really get the most out of.

To send us general feedback, simply send an e-mail to `feedback@packtpub.com`, and mention the book title via the subject of your message.

Customer support

Now that you are the proud owner of a Packt book, we have a number of things to help you to get the most from your purchase.

Downloading the example code

You can download the example code files for this book from your account at `http://www.packtpub.com`. If you purchased this book elsewhere, you can visit `http://www.packtpub.com/support` and register to have the files emailed directly to you.

You can download the code files by following these steps:

1. Log in or register to our website using your email address and password.
2. Hover the mouse pointer on the **SUPPORT** tab at the top.
3. Click on **Code Downloads & Errata**.
4. Enter the name of the book in the **Search** box.

5. Select the book for which you're looking to download the code files.
6. Choose from the drop-down menu where you purchased this book from.
7. Click on **Code Download**.

Once the file is downloaded, please make sure that you unzip or extract the folder using the latest version of:

- WinRAR / 7-Zip for Windows
- Zipeg / iZip / UnRarX for Mac
- 7-Zip / PeaZip for Linux

The code bundle for the book is also hosted on GitHub at `https://github.com/PacktPublishing/Learning-Azure-Functions`. We also have other code bundles from our rich catalog of books and videos available at `https://github.com/PacktPublishing/`. Check them out!

Downloading the color images of this book

We also provide you with a PDF file that has color images of the screenshots/diagrams used in this book. The color images will help you better understand the changes in the output. You can download this file from `https://www.packtpub.com/sites/default/files/downloads/LearningAzureFunctions_ColorImages.pdf`.

Errata

Although we have taken every care to ensure the accuracy of our content, mistakes do happen. If you find a mistake in one of our books-maybe a mistake in the text or the code-we would be grateful if you could report this to us. By doing so, you can save other readers from frustration and help us improve subsequent versions of this book. If you find any errata, please report them by visiting `http://www.packtpub.com/submit-errata`, selecting your book, clicking on the **Errata Submission Form** link, and entering the details of your errata. Once your errata are verified, your submission will be accepted and the errata will be uploaded to our website or added to any list of existing errata under the Errata section of that title.

To view the previously submitted errata, go to
`https://www.packtpub.com/books/content/support` and enter the name of the book in the
search field. The required information will appear under the **Errata** section.

Piracy

Piracy of copyrighted material on the internet is an ongoing problem across all media. At
Packt, we take the protection of our copyright and licenses very seriously. If you come
across any illegal copies of our works in any form on the internet, please provide us with
the location address or website name immediately so that we can pursue a remedy.

Please contact us at `copyright@packtpub.com` with a link to the suspected pirated
material.

We appreciate your help in protecting our authors and our ability to bring you valuable
content.

Questions

If you have a problem with any aspect of this book, you can contact us at
`questions@packtpub.com`, and we will do our best to address the problem.

1
Introducing Microsoft Azure Services and Functions

"Believe in yourself! Have faith in your abilities! Without a humble but reasonable confidence in your own powers you cannot be successful or happy."

- Norman Vincent Peale

This is an era of buzzwords. The moment we become familiar with one buzzword, another emerges and we start chasing it again. It started with cloud computing, DevOps, and now serverless computing.

This chapter introduces some of the fundamental concepts and terminology to give the reader a baseline understanding of cloud computing, cloud service models, and cloud deployment models. We will also understand what functions are and get acquainted with some of the related concepts of Microsoft Azure.

We will use a free trial of Azure Functions to get familiar with it. We will execute the sample function of printing `Hello World!` using Azure Functions.

The following are the topics that we will cover in this chapter:

- An overview of serverless architectures
- Why functions?
- An overview of Microsoft Azure services
- Azure App Services versus Azure Functions versus AWS Lambda

An overview of serverless architectures

Since the introduction of cloud computing, we have used *The Blind Men and an Elephant* story for different technology evolutions and trends. It becomes easier to convey that there is no clear definition of it and based on experience we define it differently based on our wisdom. There may not be any drastic difference but the view might be different. Reality is one, though wise men speak of it variously.

Let's understand serverless architecture by taking the story of blind men and an elephant:

According to this story of *The Blind Men and an Elephant*, the blind men decide to define an elephant by touching it and then come to their own conclusions:

- The first person placed his hand upon the elephant's trunk and said, "It feels like ... a thick snake"
- The second person placed his hand upon the elephant's ears and said, "It feels like ... a kind of fan"
- The third person placed his hand upon the elephant's legs and said, "It feels like ... a tree-trunk"
- The fourth person placed his hand upon the elephant's body and said, "It feels like ... a wall"

- The fifth person placed his hand upon the elephant's tail and said, "It feels like ... a rope"
- The sixth person placed his hand upon the elephant's tusks and said, "It feels like ... a spear"

So, there are different perspectives, but the elephant remains the same. There are many perspectives, views, and definitions available for serverless architectures or serverless computing.

Let's understand serverless architecture with respect to the evolution of computing:

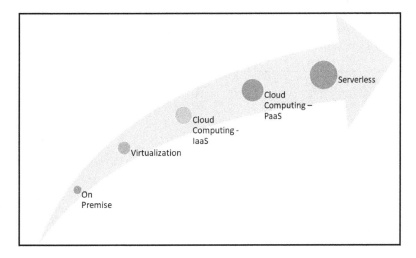

Based on the pattern of usage, the use of an on-premise resource evolved into the use of to serverless computing.

Cloud computing and service models

Change is a step-by-step process to evolve and make the existing practices more effective with enhancements. If we can find a pattern, then change/evolution is a driving force behind all path-breaking innovations. Similarly, cloud computing is a disruptive innovation in the field of infrastructure in Information Technology.

George Bernard Shaw was wise enough to say that:

"Progress is impossible without change, and those who cannot change their minds cannot change anything."

This is very appropriate for cloud computing and its adoption in the small, medium, or even large organization.

Let's understand what cloud computing is! It is no longer the elephant in the room. There are many good definitions available in the market, but I will explain what I understand and what I have experienced.

Cloud computing and its basics

Cloud computing is a kind of system that provides on-demand and agile resources in a pay-as-you-go billing model, multitenant, or dedicated computing resource such as compute, storage, and network. As per NIST definitions, cloud computing comes with four cloud deployment models and three cloud service models as given in the following diagram:

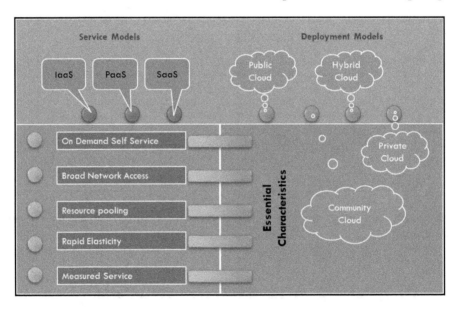

Cloud deployment models define the way resources are deployed in the environment such as on-premise and exclusively for a specific organization, that is, a private cloud; or cloud resources that are accessible to all organizations and individuals over the internet, that is, a public cloud; or cloud resources that are accessible to a specific set of organizations that share similar interests or requirements, that is, a community cloud; or cloud resources that combine two or more cloud deployment models that is known as a hybrid cloud.

There are three cloud service models that define the way cloud resources are made available to users.

Infrastructure as a Service (IaaS): Cloud resources can be **Infrastructure as a Service (IaaS)**, where the user is responsible for managing and maintaining resources/virtual machine starting, from package installation to security configuration and from upgrading packages to configuring resources for high availability as well.

Platform as a Service (PaaS): In PaaS, the cloud service provider gives flexibility to choose configuration and the user is only responsible for configuration and some troubleshooting options and monitoring options are made available by the cloud service provider.

Software as a Service (SaaS): In SaaS, the complete application is made available by the cloud service provider, where the responsibility of IaaS and PaaS remains with the cloud service provider. The user has to only use it and not worry about provisioning, monitoring, and managing the resources.

Cloud computing has few characteristics defined by NIST, which are noteworthy such as multitenancy, pay-as-you-use (similar to electricity or gas connection), on-demand self-service, resource pooling for better utilization of resources, rapid elasticity for scaling up and scaling down resources based on usage in an automated manner, and measured service for billing.

In the last few years, usage of different cloud deployment models has varied based on use cases and priorities of different organizations. Initially, a public cloud was used for noncritical applications, while a private cloud was utilized for business-critical applications, where security was a major concern. Hybrid cloud usage evolved over time with experiments, experience, and confidence in the services provided by cloud service providers.

As usual in a normal traditional environment for infrastructure management, installation, configuration, and monitoring, it was easier to adopt IaaS as there is complete control. Over time, organizations realized the pain or work behind the management of resources available in the cloud and the cost of managing resources in the cloud as the efforts are the same in managing resources considering security configurations and other configurations.

Hence, PaaS is getting popular day by day with the evolvement of Platform as a Service. PaaS has matured over the years and the scope is much wider and the services allow us to configure different programming languages such as .Net, Java, PHP, Python, and Ruby.

The following is a diagram representing different **Cloud Service Models**:

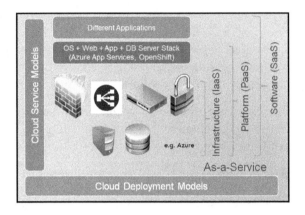

In plain English, PaaS provides an infrastructure as well as a runtime environment in combination to deploy an application. The difference is that the end user doesn't have control on the infrastructure while they can configure a runtime environment most of the time. Some service providers allow access to resources created in PaaS but not all. Features such as the ability to debug applications remotely and troubleshoot issues, up to some extent, are also provided. There are PaaS offerings, where you can have dedicated infrastructure resources for application deployment, but even in that case, control of the infrastructure is in the hands of cloud service providers.

Considering the definition of PaaS, everything is managed by the cloud service provider up to the runtime environment. For example, in the case of Java, we don't need to worry about which Java version will be installed and available to update the Java version, the web server version, and so on. Over the years, PaaS has gained its momentum and many organizations have realized that the lower the number of complexities, lesser will be the management overhead. PaaS offerings manage load balancer and high availability with little configuration and hence save lot of time and the architecture is clearer. We need to remember one thing: that most of the control lies with the cloud service provider and hence we do not have much to manage and cloud service providers have more control and they implement all best practices and standard patterns to fulfil the **service level agreements** (**SLAs**) attached with PaaS offering.

In short, those who know more about infrastructures and platforms, manage them efficiently, so we have less overhead.

Cloud service providers will handle all resource and version management of all the packages.

However, it means that it is the choice in terms of packages and other options lies with the service provider and not with the cloud consumers. Yes, cloud consumers' choices are considered based on market trends, so indirectly, users have their say in the services offered by the cloud service provider.

In a traditional environment, the infrastructure provisioning process takes place in a different manner than the acquisition of virtual machines in cloud subscription. Additionally, if there are any issues during the steps, then it takes more time in to and fro communication between different stakeholders. Let's visualize how the process workflow is executed in terms of a traditional model or in IaaS and then we will compare it with PaaS:

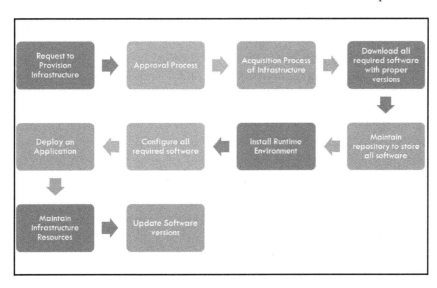

In the case of PaaS, the flow has fewer complications than the traditional or IaaS process to acquire resources as given as follows:

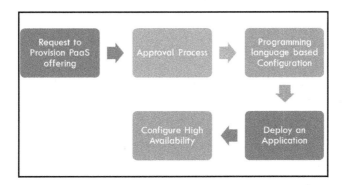

However, the approval process exists in the cloud environment too as the cost is associated with it and organizations can keep different sets of approval processes to create a virtual machine or to provision any PaaS offering such as email notification.

Having said that, there are many cloud service providers in the market that provide different types of services in an improved and innovative manner. Microsoft Azure is one of the leading cloud service providers available in the market. In the next section, we will explore some important concepts related to Microsoft Cloud to build a base of understanding on which we can kick off with Azure Functions.

Serverless computing

Serverless is not actually serverless. It means that users only need to manage code/application and not servers. The server will be managed by the service provider. We as a user only pay when our code or function is executed in the serverless or in the server that is not managed by us. Scaling is based on the request and pricing differs based on the service provider. AWS Lambda and Azure Functions are two examples of serverless computing or **Function as a Service** (**FaaS**). AWS provides a pay-as-you-go billing model, while Microsoft Azure provides a consumption plan as well as an App Service plan for Azure Functions. We will cover this in detail in a comparison table later in the chapter.

Benefits

The following are some of the benefits of serverless computing:

- Faster time to market as you can write code in the functions editor in the Azure portal and click on **Run** for execution
- No need to worry about the infrastructure and provisioning resources
- Easy bindings to services and external services
- Create functions in multiple languages as supported by the cloud service provider
- Pay only for what you use
- More cost-effective than IaaS and PaaS
- No configuration is required to set up scaling in and scaling out policies

In the next section, we will cover an overview of the Azure Functions.

Why Azure Functions?

Yes, the immediate question can be what exactly is this Azure Function? In simple English, it is running a function in a cloud environment. It enables us to create a serverless application in a Microsoft Azure environment. Consider a scenario where we know the problem, we know the code that can fix the problem, and we don't want to worry about resources that execute this code. This is the easiest way to focus on logic and business and enhancing the scope of productivity. The biggest benefit is we only need to pay for what we use. Let's understand what exactly in terms of features are provided by the Azure Functions and Azure App Services:

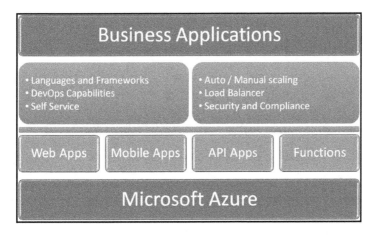

Azure App Services (Web Apps, Mobile Apps), and Functions support different languages and frameworks, DevOps capabilities, scaling, load balancer and etc.

Azure Functions is a service provided by Microsoft for serverless computing. The Azure function is a combination of code plus events plus data. Azure Functions is open source and available on GitHub:

Let's see where Azure Functions is placed in Cloud Service Models in the following figure:

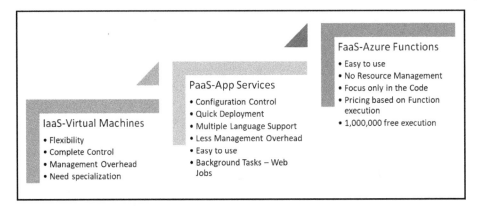

Azure Functions are similar to Azure Webjobs with some differences such as scaling policies, trigger events, and language support. We don't need to worry about infrastructure for execution of the piece of code or function. It is like a FaaS. We can execute Azure Functions in response to events as well.

The languages that are supported are C#, F#, Node.js, Python or PHP, batch, bash, or PowerShell.

There are two types of pricing plans available in the Azure Functions:

1. **Consumption plan**: When we execute functions, Microsoft Azure provides all the resources. We don't need to worry about resource management, and we only pay for the time that our functions are executed. The consumption plan pricing includes a monthly free grant of 1 million requests and 400,000 GBs of resource consumption per month. Free grants apply to paid consumption subscriptions only.
2. **App Service plan**: This executes functions just the way we execute Azure App Services. We can utilize the same App Service plan created for any application and execute Azure Functions on it without any extra cost.

Having App Service plan as the host for Azure Functions provides lots of benefits that are available with Azure App Services. We can utilize remote debugging, deployment slots, continuous deployment, vertical scaling and horizontal scaling, auto-scaling, and so on. If we use the Azure App Service, then it is a multitenant scenario. If we want to utilize a dedicated environment, then we can utilize the App Service Environment that is a dedicated service from Microsoft Azure, where we can host a function in a virtual network and configure **network security groups** (**NSGs**) for an enhanced level of security.

Triggers and bindings are the core of Azure Functions. It allows us to write a function to respond to events that occur in the Azure or other services. As the name suggests, trigger indicates how the function should be invoked and bindings are related to data. Azure Functions can have only one trigger associated with it. Bindings are the connection to the data from within the code available in the function. Unlike triggers, functions can have one or more input and output bindings.

The following table shows the triggers and bindings that are supported with Azure Functions:

Type	Service	Trigger*	Input	Output
Schedule	Azure Functions	Yes		
HTTP (REST or Webhook)	Azure Functions	Yes		Yes**
Blob Storage	Azure Storage	Yes	Yes	Yes
Events	Azure Event Hubs	Yes		Yes
Queues	Azure Storage	Yes		Yes
Queues and topics	Azure Service Bus	Yes		Yes
Storage tables	Azure Storage		Yes	Yes
SQL tables	Azure Mobile Apps		Yes	Yes
No-SQL DB	Azure DocumentDB		Yes	Yes
Push Notifications	Azure Notification Hubs			Yes
Twilio SMS Text	Twilio			Yes
SendGrid email	SendGrid			Yes

(* - All triggers have associated input data)

 (** - The HTTP output binding requires an HTTP trigger)

Let's try to get to grips with Azure Functions quickly:

1. Go to `https://functions.azure.com/try`.
2. Select **Webhook + API** as a scenario and select **JavaScript** as the language.
3. Click on **Create this function**:

4. Select an auth provider.

5. Select any suitable authentication method and sign in with it:

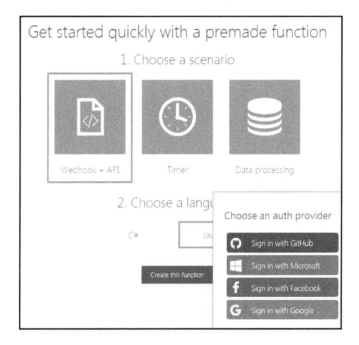

6. Wait for few seconds until a free trial fo Azure Functions is ready:

7. The sample script is ready for `Hello World!`:

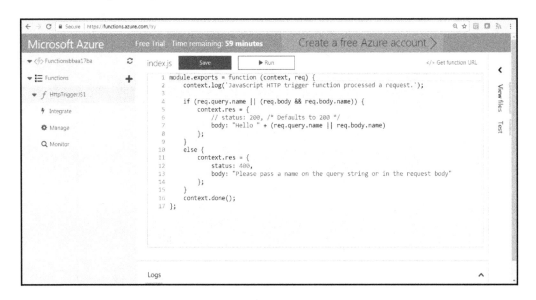

8. Click on **Test** on the right side of the browser window. In **Request body**, provide the **name**:

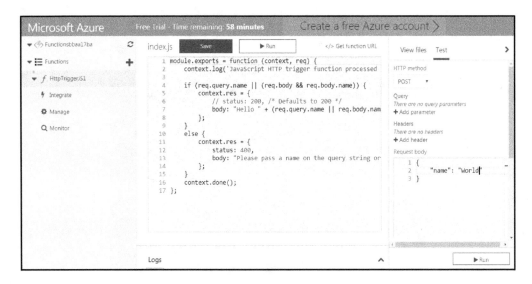

9. Click on **Run** and scroll down.

10. See the **Output** and **Status**:

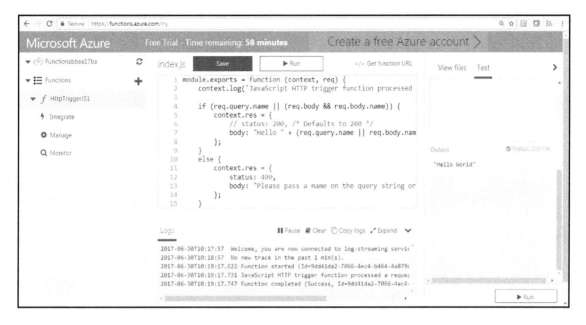

So, we have just executed the simple Hello World function. We will execute Azure Functions in a proper Azure subscription in later chapters.

The following are some of the benefits of Azure Functions:

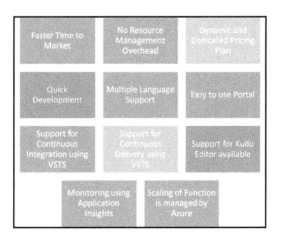

Before we jump to Azure Functions, let's understand some basics of Microsoft Azure cloud. We will discuss the key components and services of Microsoft Azure in the next section.

An overview of Microsoft Azure Services

Microsoft Azure falls into the category of a public cloud deployment model when we consider the definition of cloud computing by the **National Institute of Standards and Technology** (**NIST**). Let's first understand the different services of Microsoft Azure and some of the terminology that will be useful later in the book.

Microsoft Azure provides different kinds of services based on different use cases. Let's understand the core concepts to make our foundation robust.

Microsoft Azure comes up with some core concepts that are important to understand before we go ahead and work with it. These core concepts helps us to manage resources and understand the pricing structure as well.

Regions

Microsoft Azure services are available in 34 regions around the globe and they are continuously planning to support more regions. The more regions, the greater the number of customers allowed to achieve better performance with cost optimization. It also helps in the scenarios where data location is legally restricted.

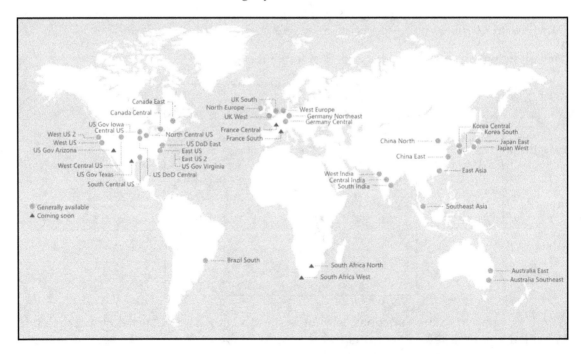

To get the latest details on Microsoft Azure regions, visit
`https://azure.microsoft.com/en-in/regions/`.

To verify Azure Functions available by region, go to
`https://azure.microsoft.com/en-in/regions/services/` and check the **Functions**
section:

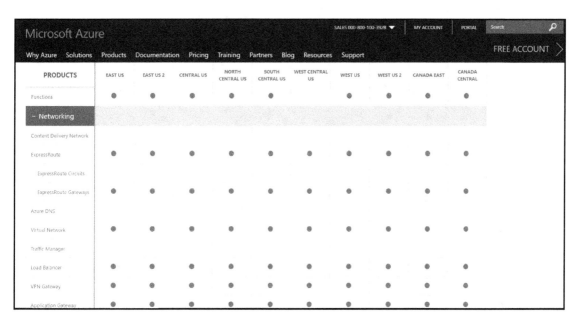

Azure is generally available in 34 regions and 12 **Graphic Environment Operating Systems**
(**GEOSs**) around the globe. It has already announced plans for 6 additional regions and 2
additional GEOSs. For customers, it is extremely important to have legal compliance in the
context of storage location of their data. There are two different possibilities/authorities in
this scenario:

1. Customers may copy, move, or access data from any location

2. Microsoft may replicate data in other regions of the same GEO for high availability:

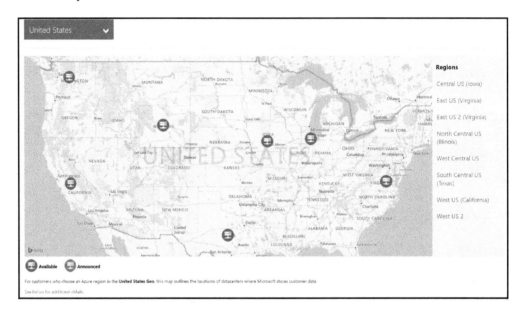

To get more details, go to
`http://azuredatacentermap.azurewebsites.net/`.

Resource groups

Resource groups in Microsoft Azure are logical containers. A resource group is useful for managing resources and providing role-based access to all the resources available in the group easily. It can be used to group all different resources such as App Services, SQL databases, and storage accounts available in Microsoft Azure. We will consider services that we will use in this chapter for most of the examples.

For example, we need to create resources such as Azure Web Apps, SQL database, and a storage account in West US and provide access to some users. It is painful to assign users to individual resources. Rather, it is more manageable if we can provide group access to all the resources.

This way the resources can be managed in a better way.

1. To create a resource group, go to Azure Portal `https://portal.azure.com` and click on **Resource Groups** in the left sidebar menu.
2. Click on **+ Add** to create a resource group.
3. Provide the **Resource group name**, select **Subscription**, select **Resource group location**, and then click on **Create**:

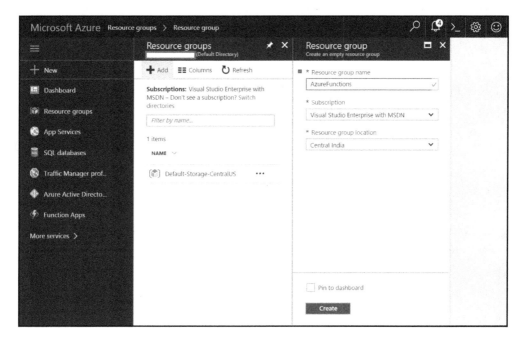

4. Wait until the resource group is created:

5. Click on the **AzureFunctions** resource group:

6. Once the **AzureFunctions</span resource group is created, click on it and verify the Overview section. As of now, there are no resources in the resource group, hence there are No deployments in the Overview section and No resources to display:

7. To provide role-based access, click on **Access control (IAM)**. Check the **OWNER** and other details:

8. Click on **+ Add** and select **Contributor** role. Find the member whom you want to give access to this resource group:

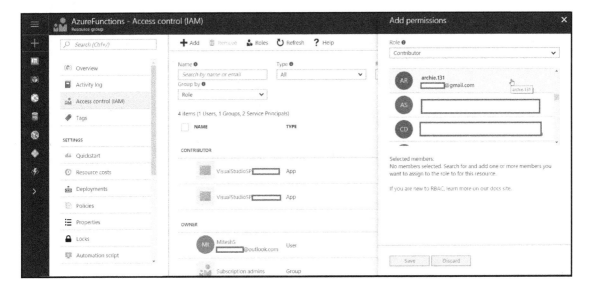

9. Select the member and click on **Save**:

We will use this resource group in the coming chapters as a logical container for different resources such as Azure Functions and storage.

App Services - Microsoft Azure Web Apps

Microsoft Azure App Services is one of the most popular offering from Microsoft Azure. It is a PaaS. There are four kinds of applications created in App services:

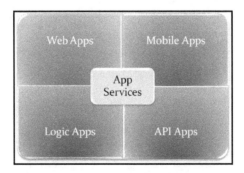

Azure App Services is a PaaS offering that has computing resources and runtime environments managed by Microsoft Azure, while the user is only responsible for applications and configurations relating to Web App and High Availability.

The following are some quick points about Azure Web Apps:

- App Services run on virtual machines - virtual machines are managed by Microsoft Azure
- There are five pricing tiers that are available - Free, Shared, Basic, Standard, and Premium
- It supports applications written in Java, ASP.NET, PHP, Node.js, and Python
- We can integrate Apps with Visual Studio or GitHub
- We can create Apps from the Azure portal and also from the command line using Powershell commands; hence, it is easier to automate the creation process
- We can set Continuous Integration and Continuous Delivery or Deployment using Build and Release of Visual Studio Team Services
- We can configure auto-scaling and make it available across the regions; we can set high availability as well

Let's look at some basic differences between Azure Virtual Machines and Azure Web Apps:

	Microsoft Azure Virtual Machines	**Microsoft Azure Web Apps**
Offering	Infrastructure as a Service	Platform as a Service
Support	Support for Linux, Windows Server, SQL Server, Oracle, IBM, and SAP	Linux and Windows
Categories	General Purpose Compute Optimized Memory Optimized GPU High Performance Compute	Free Share Basic Standard Premium
Cost	Per minute billing	Per minute billing
Virtual Infrastructure Responsibility	User	Microsoft Azure
Out of the Box support for VSTS	No	Yes
Management Overhead	Yes	No

Installation and Configuration required?	Yes; the customer is responsible for managing the resources	Web Apps come with a platform that supports different programming languages; we only need to configure the Application settings

App Service plan

An **App Service plan** (**ASP**) is a combination of capacities (instance size and instance count on which the application is hosted) and features. Capacity is directly related to cost and hence it is similar to choosing a pricing tier. There are different capabilities and limits available in pricing plans.

Each ASP can be used for different purposes and they provide different features too. There are five pricing tiers as follows:

- **Free**: no scaling
- **Shared**: no scaling
- **Basic**: SLA - 99.95%; maximum instances for scaling - 3
- **Standard**: SLA - 99.95%; autoscale, 5 deployment slots; Geo-distributed deployment, VPN hybrid connectivity, deployment slots, and automated backups; maximum instances for scaling - 10
- **Premium**: SLA - 99.95%; 20 deployment slots; autoscale, geo-distributed deployment, VPN hybrid connectivity, deployment slots, and automated backups; maximum instances for scaling - 50

 App Service or Azure Web App is the main production slot. In the standard and premium tiers, we can create other deployment slots other than the main slot in which we deploy the application. We can use deployment slots for different environments before deploying applications into the main slot. Slots are not different from a live web app. They have their own set of content and configurations and hostnames. We can swap slots to roll back failures too.

The following are some important points regarding an App Service plan:

- An App Service plan can be shared by multiple applications.
- Deployment slots are usually deployed on the same App Service plan.
- Azure Web Apps configured with an App Service plan are changed, and then these changes affect all the applications hosted on the App Service plan.

- By default, ASP comes with a single instance. If we increase the instance count, then the applications hosted on a single instance will be hosted on other instances too.
- The number of instances in ASP is directly associated with the price of Azure Web Apps.

Let's create an App Service plan in Microsoft Azure Portal:

1. Click on **More services** in the left sidebar and find **App Service plans**.
2. Click on **+ Add**.
3. Provide the **App Service plan** name, **Subscription**, **Resource Group**, **Operating System**, **Location** and **Pricing tier**, and then click on **Create**:

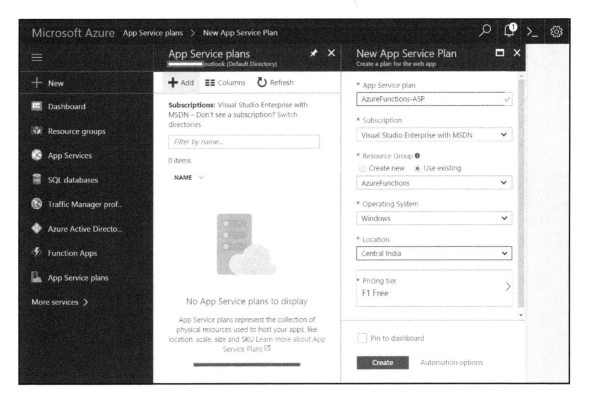

4. Click on **Notifications** to get the progress details of the App Service plan deployment:

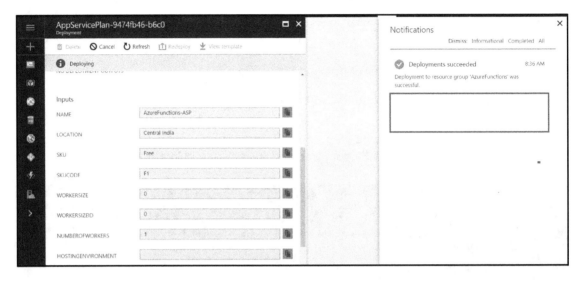

5. Once App Service plan is created successfully, click on the **Overview** section to get details about it in the Azure Portal:

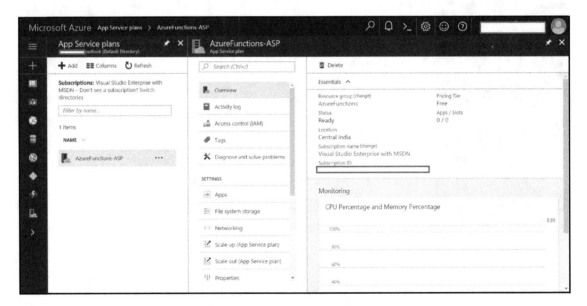

We can deploy Azure App Services or Azure Functions on App Service plan.

Azure Active Directory

Azure Active Directory (**Azure AD**) is a cloud based, multitenant, and highly available identity management service from Microsoft:

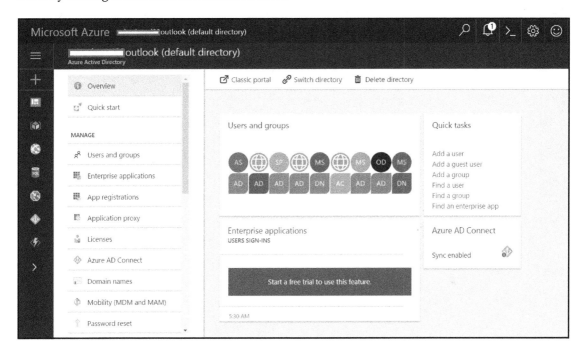

We can manage users, groups, multifactor authentication, add an application that an organization is developing for authentication, add an application from the gallery for authentication, add a custom domain, role based access control, and so on:

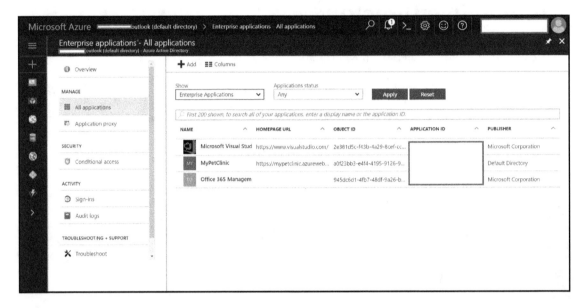

Application Gallery supports more than 2500 applications at the time of writing this chapter:

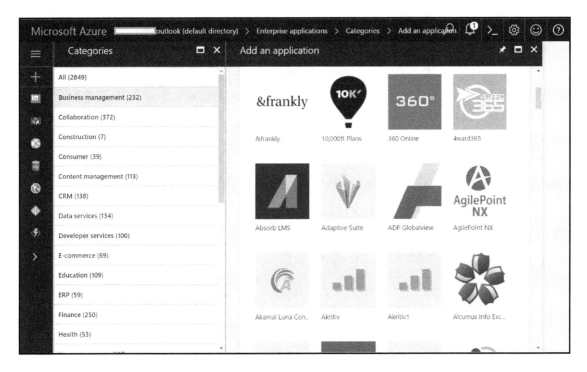

The categories include business management, collaboration, construction, content management, CRM, data services, developer services, e-commerce, education, ERP, finance, health, human resources, IT infrastructure, mail, marketing, media, mobile device management, productivity, project management, security, social, supply management, telecommunications, travel, and web design and hosting.

App Insights

Application Insights is a flexible analytics service. It helps us to get insights of performance and usage of application. It can be used for .NET or J2EE-based applications that are hosted on-premises or in the cloud. Let's create Application Insights for a sample application:

1. Create a sample application and go to its **Monitoring** section. Click on **Application Insights**. Select **Create new resource** and click on **OK**.

2. We can create a Web test for testing application availability from multiple regions. We can select a ping test or a multistep test to check the availability, and alert criteria can also be configured.

3. Performance Testing is also a very interesting feature available in App Insights. It is more of a load test based on the number of users over a specific duration.

4. We will see the **how to** of both in this book, where we intend to cover monitoring.

Azure Services versus AzureFunctions versus AWS Lambda

Let's try to compare Azure App Services, Azure Functions, and AWS Lambda. The following table may not contain all the points:

	Azure App Services	Azure Functions	AWS Lambda
Category	Platform as a Service.	Allows you to develop serverless applications on Microsoft Azure.	Allows you to develop serverless applications on AWS.
Definition	Microsoft Azure App Service is a PaaS offering. We can create web and mobile apps for any platform or device.	Azure Functions is a service provided by Microsoft to run small pieces of code, or functions, in the Microsoft Azure cloud. We only need to focus on the problem and not the resources required for the solution.	AWS Lambda allows us to execute code in serverless architecture, where the resources are managed by AWS.
Vendor	Microsoft Azure.	Microsoft Azure.	Amazon/AWS.
Available from	2015.	2016.	2014.
Languages Supported	ASP.NET, Node.js, Java, PHP, and Python.	C#, F#, Node.js, Python, PHP, batch, bash, or any executable.	Node.js (JavaScript), Python, Java (Java 8 compatible), and C# (.NET Core).
Integrated development environment support	Yes (Microsoft Visual Studio IDE).	Yes (Visual Studio).	Yes (Eclipse IDE and Visual Studio IDE).
Environment variables support	Yes, in Application Settings.	Yes.	Yes.
Cost	App Service plan can be hosted are FREE (try for free), SHARED (host basic apps), BASIC (more features for Dev / Test), STANDARD (go live with web and mobile), and PREMIUM (enterprise scale and integration). For more details go to https://azure.microsoft.com/en-in/pricing/details/app-service/.	Consumption plan means that when we execute functions, Microsoft Azure provides all the resources. We don't need to worry about resource management, and we only pay for the time that our function runs. For more details go to https://azure.microsoft.com/en-in/pricing/details/functions/.	The Lambda free tier includes 1M free requests per month and 400,000 GB-seconds of compute time per month. The first 1 million requests per month are free and $0.20 per 1 million requests thereafter ($0.0000002 per request). For more details go to https://aws.amazon.com/lambda/pricing/.
Eligible for free tier	Yes.	Yes.	Yes.
Flexibility in configuration of resources	Yes.	Limited. (If App Service plan is used then configuration of resources is available.)	No (need to verify).
Execution time	N/A.	Azure Function must complete execution within 300 seconds.	AWS Lambda function must complete execution within 300 seconds.
Limit to the number of functions that can be executed	N/A.	No.	No.
Concurrent executions	N/A.	No limit.	By default, AWS Lambda limits the total concurrent executions across all functions within a given region to 1000.
Scalability	Manual and automatic scaling available in the form of an App Service plan.	Manual and automatic scaling has two plans available for costing; a Consumption plan and an App Service plan. For more details, check the Cost section in this comparison table.	Automatic scaling.
Monitoring	Azure App Insights / Azure App Service Default Monitoring.	N/A	Amazon CloudWatch console or AWS Lambda console.

Templates	Web Web + SQL Web Apps Mobile Apps Logic Apps Media services Blogs + CMSs Starter web apps Web app frameworks Ecommerce Add-ons	BlobTrigger EventHubTrigger Generic Webhook GitHub Webhook HTTPTrigger QueueTrigger ServiceBusQueueTrigger ServiceBusTopicTrigger TimerTrigger	Blank function kinesis-firehose-syslog-to-json alexa-skill-kit-sdk-factskill batch-get-job-python27 kinesis-firehose-apachelog-to-json cloudfront-modify-response-heade s3-get-object-python config-rule-change-triggered lex-book-trip-python
Supported event sources /integrations	N/A.	Azure Cosmos DB Azure Event Hubs Azure Mobile Apps (tables) Azure Notification Hubs Azure Service Bus (queues and topics) Azure Storage (blob, queues, and tables) GitHub (Webhooks) On-premises (using Service Bus) Twilio (SMS messages)	Amazon S3 Amazon DynamoDB Amazon Kinesis Streams Amazon Simple Notification Service Amazon Simple Email Service Amazon Cognito AWS CloudFormation Amazon CloudWatch Logs Amazon CloudWatch Events AWS CodeCommit Scheduled Events (powered by Amazon CloudWatch Events) AWS Config Amazon Alexa Amazon Lex Amazon API Gateway Other Event Sources: Invoking a Lambda Function On Demand Sample Events Published by Event Sources
URL	https://azure.microsoft.com/en-us/services/app-service/	https://azure.microsoft.com/en-us/services/functions/	https://aws.amazon.com/lambda/
Documentation	https://docs.microsoft.com/en-us/azure/app-service/	https://docs.microsoft.com/en-us/azure/azure-functions/	https://aws.amazon.com/documentation/lambda/

Summary

So finally, we are at the end of the first chapter of this book.

In this chapter, we have discussed serverless architecture with the evolution of cloud computing. We covered the definition of cloud computing, cloud service models, cloud deployment models, and so on.

We discussed in detail about IaaS and PaaS and how they have matured and how the use cases have changed and why. We touched upon serverless computing and its visible benefits as an evolution.

We also discussed in detail Azure Function, saw an overview of how the function is executed in a free trial, and got a basic understanding of the Microsoft Azure platform.

In the last section of this chapter, we covered some of the differences between Web App AWS Lambda and Azure Functions.

In the next chapter, we will discuss Azure Functions, its architecture, and other details and we will create our first function in the Microsoft Azure subscription.

2
First Function App - Anatomy and Structure of a Function App

"Where there is a will, there is a way. If there is a chance in a million that you can do something, anything, to keep what you want from ending, do it. Pry the door open or, if need be, wedge your foot in that door and keep it open."

- Pauline Kael

There is always a first time for everything. Here in this chapter, we will take one scenario and then we will try to complete the scenario with Azure Functions so that we can understand how Azure Functions work, and the different resources of Microsoft Azure that are involved in the whole scenario.

In this chapter, we will focus on creating our first Azure Function. We will create an Azure Function App and then we will create an Azure Function with triggers and output bindings.

We will also troubleshoot if we find any issues in the Azure Function. One of the most important things in Azure App Services or Azure Functions is the Kudu editor.

We will go through in detail about the Kudu editor, folder structure, and files available in the Azure Functions.

In this chapter, we will cover following topics:

- Anatomy of Azure Functions
- Setting up a basic Azure Function
- Troubleshooting Azure Functions
- Executing the Azure Function

Anatomy of Azure Functions

Let's understand the different components or resources that are used while creating Azure Functions.

The following image describes the Functions in Azure in different pricing plans:

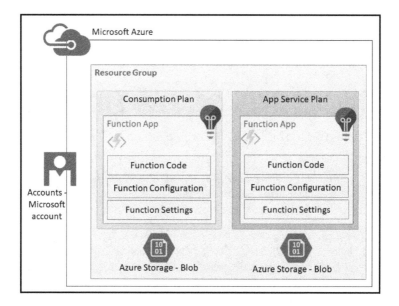

Azure Function App

A function app is a collection of one or more functions that are managed together. All the functions in a Function App share the same pricing plan and it can be a consumption plan or an App Service plan. When we utilize Visual Studio Team Services for Continuous Integration and Continuous Delivery using build and release definitions, then the Function app is also shared. The way we manage different resources in Azure with the Azure Resource Group is similar to how we can manage multiple functions with the Function App.

Function code

In this chapter, we will consider a scenario where a photography competition is held and photographers need to upload photographs to the portal. The moment a photograph is uploaded, a thumbnail should be created immediately.

A function code is the main content that executes and performs some operations as shown as follows:

```
var Jimp = require("jimp");

// JavaScript function must export a single function via module.exports
// To find the function and execute it

module.exports = (context, myBlob) => {
// context is a must have parameter and first parameter always
// context is used to pass data to and from the function
//context name is not fixed; it can be anything

    // Read Photograph with Jimp
    Jimp.read(myBlob).then((image) => {
        // Manipulate Photograph
      // resize the Photograph. Jimp.AUTO can be passed as one of the
values.
        image
            .resize(200, 200)
            .quality(40)
            .getBuffer(Jimp.MIME_JPEG, (error, stream) => {
                // Check for errors while processing the Photograph.
                if (error) {
                // To print the message on log console
                    context.log('There was an error processing the
Photograph.');
                    // To communicate with the runtime that function is finished
to avoid timeout
                    context.done(error);
                }
                else {
                // To print the message on log console
                    context.log('Successfully processed the Photograph');
                    // To communicate with the runtime that function is
finished to avoid timeout
                    // Bind the stream to the output binding to create a new
blob
                    context.done(null, stream);
                }
            });
    });
};
```

Function configuration

Function configuration defines the function bindings and other configuration settings. It contains configurations such as the type of trigger, paths for blob containers, and so on:

```
{
  "bindings": [
    {
      "name": "myBlob",
      "type": "blobTrigger",
      "direction": "in",
      "path": "photographs/{name}",
      "connection": "origphotography2017_STORAGE",
      "dataType": "binary"
    },
    {
      "type": "blob",
      "name": "$return",
      "path": "thumbnails/{name}",
      "connection": "origphotography2017_STORAGE",
      "direction": "out"
    }
  ],
  "disabled": false
}
```

The function runtime uses this configuration file to decide which events to monitor and how to pass data to and from the function execution.

Function settings

We can limit the daily usage quota and application settings. We can enable Azure Function proxies and change the edit mode of our function app. The application settings in the Function App are similar to the application settings in Azure App Services. We can configure .NET Framework v4.6, Java version, Platform, ARR Affinity, remote debugging, remote Visual Studio version, app settings, and connection strings.

Runtime

The runtime is responsible for executing function code on the underlying WebJobs SDK host.

In the next section, we will create our Function App and functions using the Azure Portal and execute them.

Setting up a basic Azure Function

Let's understand Azure Functions and create one in Azure Portal.

1. Go to `https://portal.azure.com`. Click on **Function Apps** in the left sidebar:

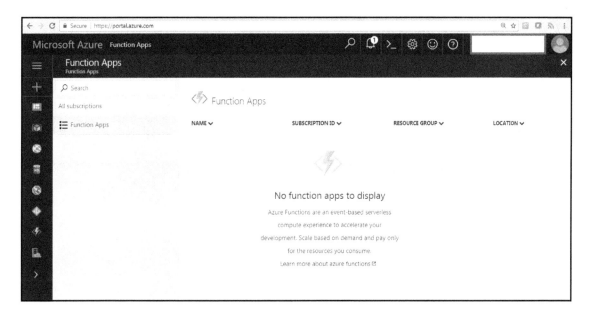

There is no Function App available as of now.

2. Click on the *plus* + sign and search for **Function Apps**. Then click on **Create**:

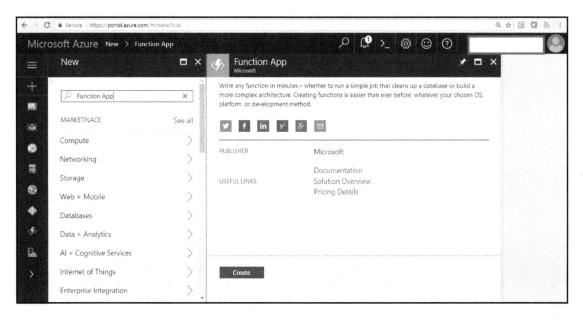

3. Provide the **App name**, **Subscription** details, and existing **Resource Group**. Select **Consumption Plan** in **Hosting Plan**. Then select **Location**:

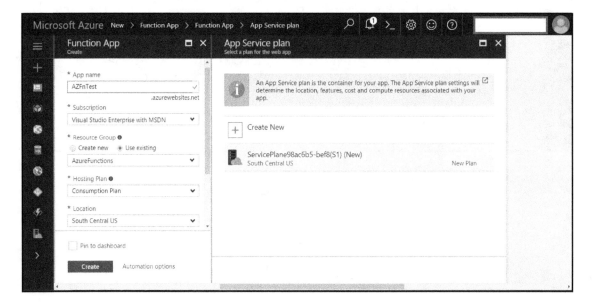

4. Select **Create New** in **Storage** and click on **Create**:

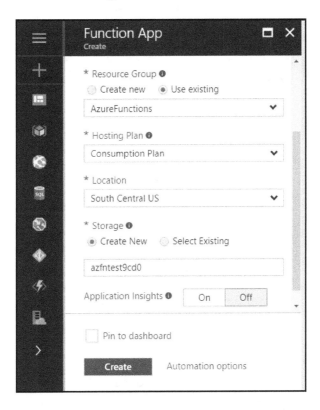

5. Now, let's go to **Function Apps** in the left sidebar and verify whether the recently created Function App is available in the list or not:

6. Click on the Function App and we can see the details related to the **Subscription**, **Resource group, URL, Location, App Service Plan / pricing tier**.

We can stop or restart the function from the same pane.

7. The **Settings** tab provides details on the **Runtime version**, **Application settings**, and the limit on daily usage:

It also allows us to keep the Function App in **Read/Write** or **Read Only** mode. We can also enable deployment slots, a well-known feature of Azure App Services:

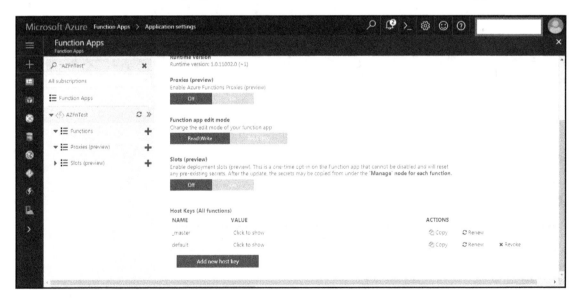

8. In the **Platform features** tab as shown below, we get different kinds of options to enable the Function App with **MONITORING, NETWORKING, DEPLOYMENT TOOLS**, and so on. We will cover most of the features in this chapter and in upcoming chapters in detail:

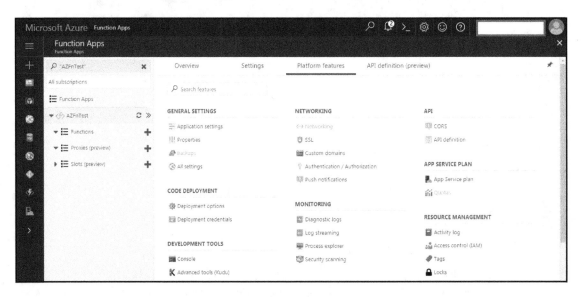

9. Click on **Properties**. Verify the different details that are available:

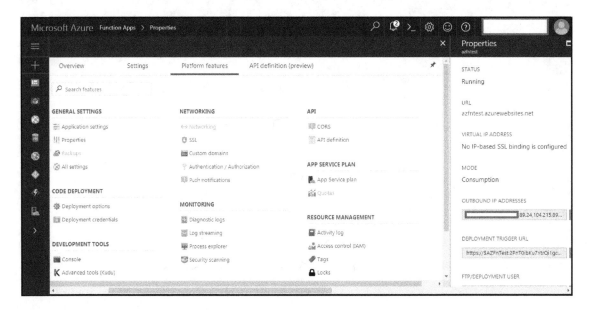

There is a property named **OUTBOUND IP ADDRESSES** which is useful if we need the IP addresses of the Function App for whitelisting.

10. Click on **App Service plan** and it will open a consumption plan in the pane:

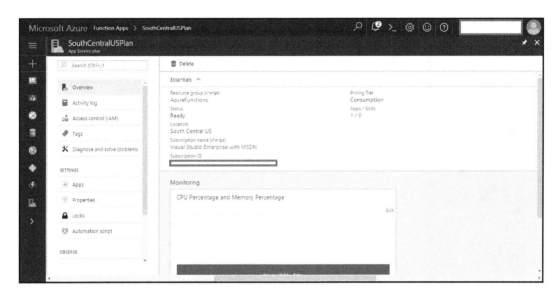

11. On the left sidebar in the Azure Portal, go to **Storage** services and verify the storage accounts that are available:

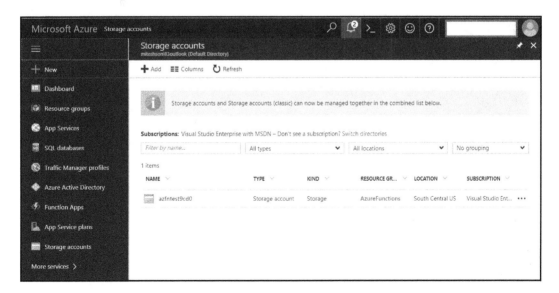

What we want to achieve is that when we upload an image in a specific blob container, the function should be available immediately in the Function App and should be executed and create a thumbnail in another blob container.

12. Create a new storage account:

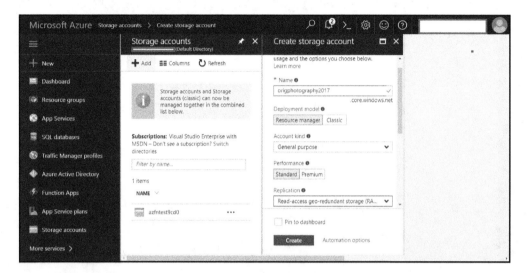

13. Go to the **Overview** section of the **Storage accounts** and check all the available settings:

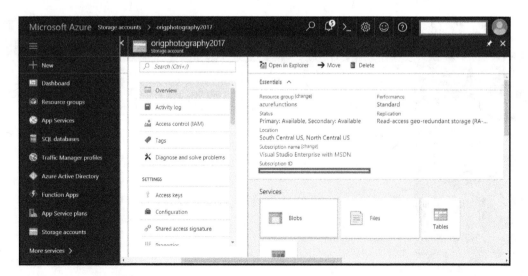

14. Click on the **Containers** section in the **Storage accounts**:

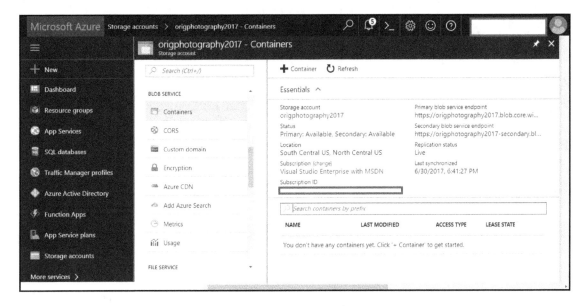

There is no container available in the **Storage accounts**.

15. Click on **+ Container** and fill in the **Name** and **Access type** and click on **OK**:

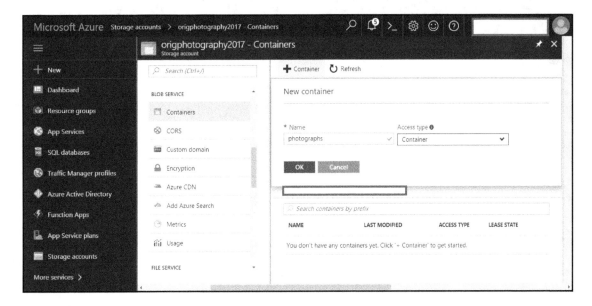

16. Similarly, create another container to store thumbnails:

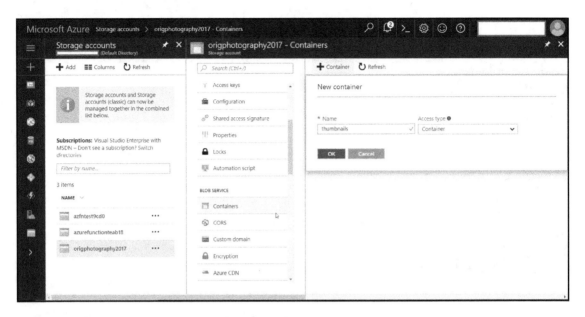

17. Verify both containers in the **Storage accounts**:

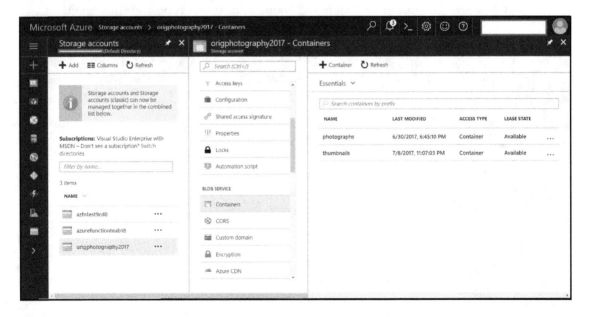

Once we have all the components ready to achieve our main objective of creating a function that creates thumbnails of photographs, we can start creating a function:

1. Click on the **Functions** section in the Function App:

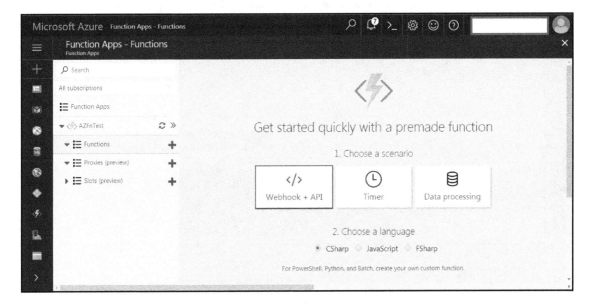

2. Select **Webhook + API** and then choose a language:

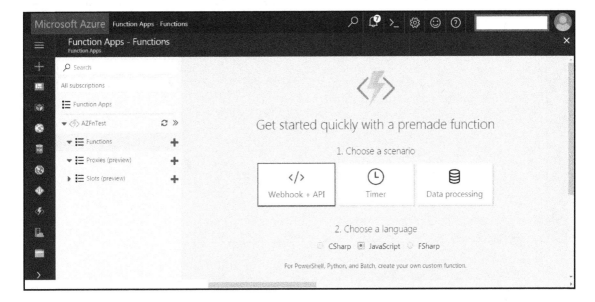

3. Click on **Custom function** so that we can utilize the already available templates:

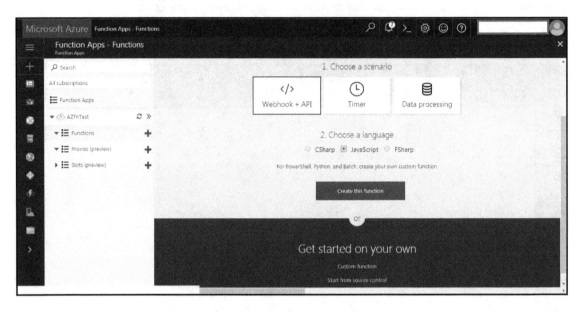

4. Select the **Language** as **JavaScript**:

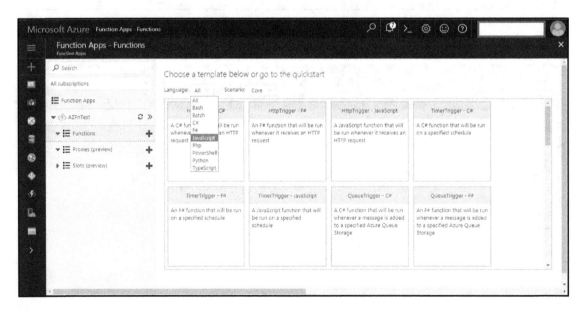

5. Select the **BlobTrigger** template:

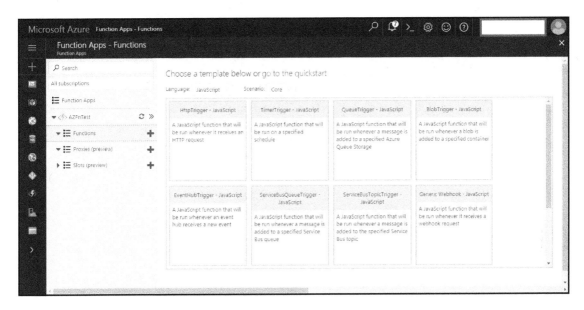

6. Provide the name of our function.
7. Give the path to the container for the source and select **Storage account connection**:

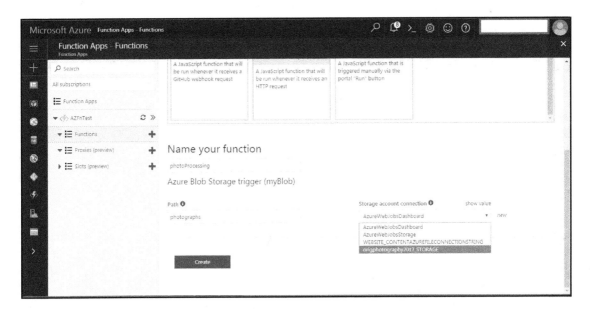

8. Look at the function and code available in the code editor in the Microsoft Azure Portal:

Before we write the actual code in the function, let's configure the triggers and outputs:

1. Select **Blob parameter name**, **Storage account connection**, and **Path**:

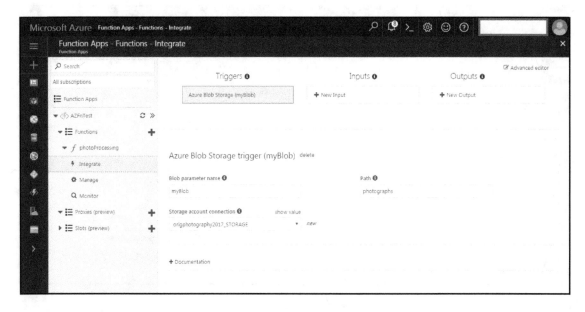

2. Click on **New Output**.
3. Select **Azure Blob Storage**:

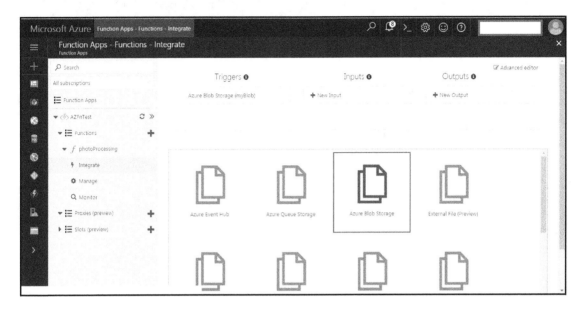

4. Select **Blob parameter name**, **Storage account connection**, and **Path**.
5. Click on **Save**:

6. Review the final output bindings:

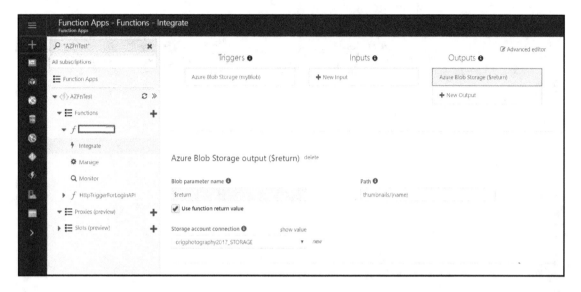

7. Click on the advanced editor link to review **function.json**:

8. Now, paste the function code for creating a thumbnail into the **Functions** code editor:

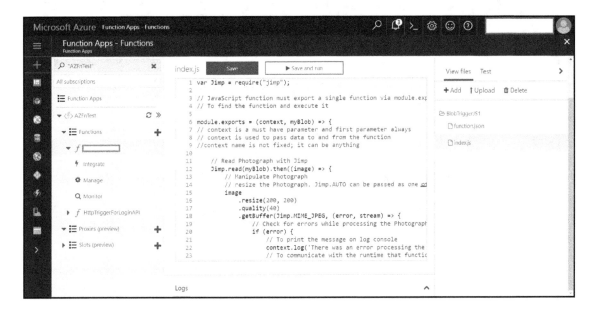

Now, once everything is set and configured, let's upload a photograph in the photographs blob container:

1. Click on the container and click on **Upload**. Select the photograph that needs to be uploaded to the container.

2. Click on **Upload**:

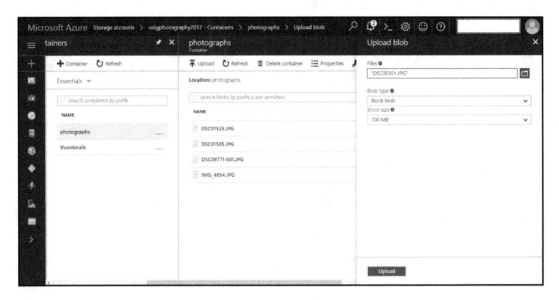

3. Go to **Function Apps** and check the logs.

4. We may get an Error: **Cannot find module 'jimp'**:

```
2017-06-30T16:54:18 Welcome, you are now connected to log-
streaming service.
2017-06-30T16:54:41.202 Script for function 'photoProcessing'
changed. Reloading.
2017-06-30T16:55:01.309 Function started
(Id=411e4d84-5ef0-4ca9-b963-ed94c0ba8e84)
2017-06-30T16:55:01.371 Function completed (Failure,
Id=411e4d84-5ef0-4ca9-b963-ed94c0ba8e84, Duration=59ms)
2017-06-30T16:55:01.418 Exception while executing function:
Functions.photoProcessing. mscorlib: Error: Cannot find module
'jimp'
at Function.Module._resolveFilename (module.js:455:15)
at Function.Module._load (module.js:403:25)
at Module.require (module.js:483:17)
at require (internal/module.js:20:19)
at Object.<anonymous>
(D:\home\site\wwwroot\photoProcessing\index.js:1:74)
at Module._compile (module.js:556:32)
at Object.Module._extensions..js (module.js:565:10)
at Module.load (module.js:473:32)
at tryModuleLoad (module.js:432:12)
at Function.Module._load (module.js:424:3).
```

In the next section, we will troubleshoot this issue.

Troubleshooting Azure Functions

Let's troubleshoot the issue we faced while executing the Azure Function.

1. Go to the **Kudu** console of the Azure Function App.
2. Click on **Debug Console** and select **Powershell**.
3. Execute the `npm install -save jimp` command:

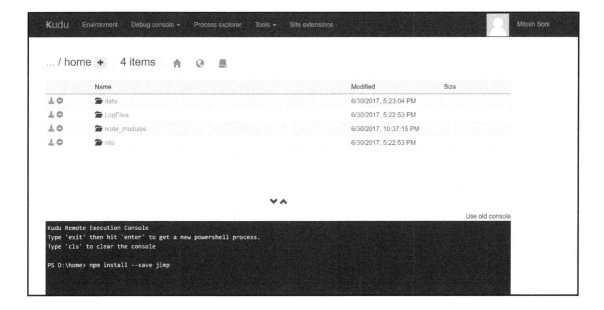

4. Once the command execution has completed successfully, go to the `node_modules` directory and review the `jimp` module in this directory:

5. Understand the folder structure of a function in the Kudu editor. Click on the **Debug Console** and select **Powershell**:

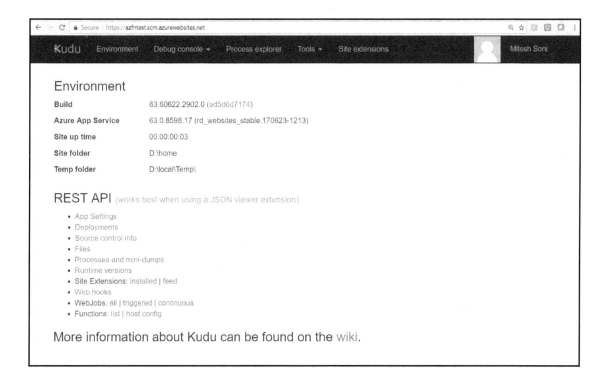

6. Click on the `node_modules` directory to review all the modules available for usage:

7. There are many modules available for the Azure Functions to utilize:

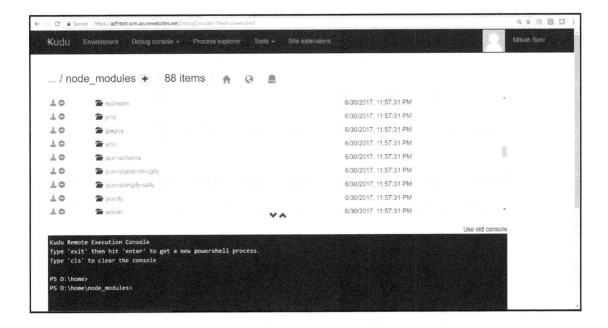

1. Click on the site in the Kudu editor. Go to `www.root` and select the function name to review which files are available in the specific function.

2. As we saw in the Azure Portal, we can also see `function.json` and `index.js`:

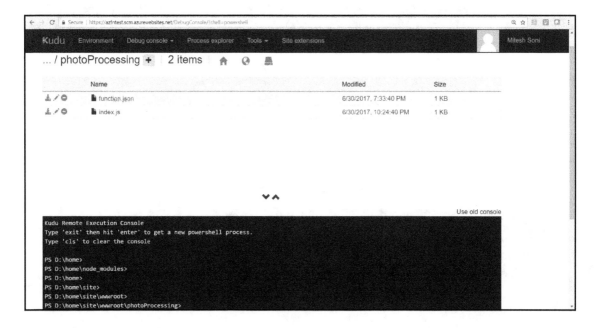

10. Click on the *edit* icon of `function.json`:

```
Kudu    Environment    Debug console ▾    Process explorer    Tools ▾    Site extensions                    Mitesh Soni

Save     Cancel    |    function.json

 1 ▾ {
 2 ▾     "bindings": [
 3 ▾         {
 4              "name": "myBlob",
 5              "type": "blobTrigger",
 6              "direction": "in",
 7              "path": "photographs/{name}",
 8              "connection": "origphotography2017_STORAGE",
 9              "dataType": "binary"
10          },
11 ▾         {
12              "type": "blob",
13              "name": "$return",
14              "path": "thumbnails/{name}",
15              "connection": "origphotography2017_STORAGE",
16              "direction": "out"
17          }
18      ],
19      "disabled": false
20  }
```

In the next section, we will try to execute the Azure Function again by uploading a photograph to a blob container.

Executing the Azure Function

Now, let's try to upload a photo to the photographs blob container that we created earlier.

Once the photograph is uploaded, go to Function Apps and verify the logs:

2017-07-09T11:03:11 Welcome, you are now connected to log-streaming service.

2017-07-09T11:04:11 No new trace in the past 1 min(s).

2017-07-09T11:05:11 No new trace in the past 2 min(s).

2017-07-09T11:05:11.656 Function started (Id=e3f715fa-da5b-4cf6-9ada-410ec8db956a)

2017-07-09T11:06:53.592 Successfully processed the Photograph

2017-07-09T11:06:53.686 Function completed (Success, Id=e3f715fa-da5b-4cf6-9ada-410ec8db956a, Duration=102034ms)

2017-07-09T11:08:11 No new trace in the past 1 min(s).

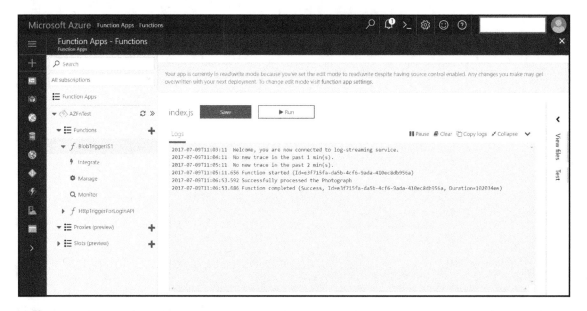

Check that the photograph has uploaded in the photographs container:

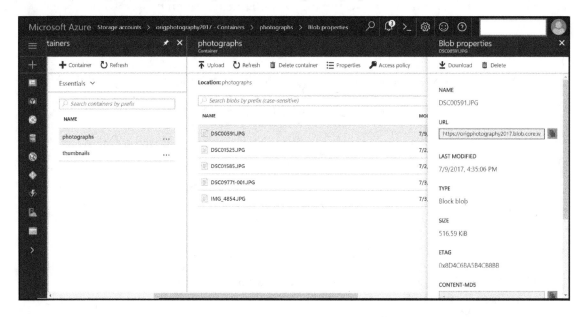

Check that the photograph has uploaded in the thumbnails container and verify the size of the photograph:

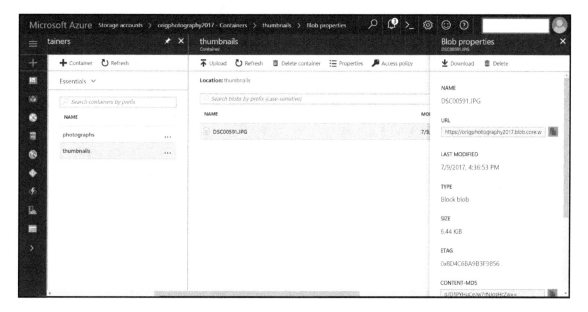

To know the status of the Azure Function App, visit the URL given in Azure Portal and we will get the details as shown in the following screenshot:

So finally, we have created one function that is invoked when a photograph is uploaded to the blob container in the Azure Storage.

Summary

Finally, we have created our first function that processes a photograph and creates a thumbnail for a photography competition scenario.

We have also seen the anatomy of Azure Functions and covered the troubleshooting of issues that can occur in the Azure Function processing.

So, we have covered all the basic things to execute a simple function with triggers and output binding.

In the next chapter, we will discuss triggers in detail.

3
Application of Triggers

"The difference between ordinary and extraordinary is that little extra."

- Jimmy Johnson

First, let's understand what a trigger is.

In normal English, a trigger is an event or situation that causes something to start. This something can be some sort of processing of data or some other service that performs some action. Triggers are just a set of functions that get executed when some event gets fired.

In Azure, we have different types of triggers, such as an implicit trigger, and we can also create a manual trigger.

Azure Functions allow you to write code in response to a trigger in Azure. As we have seen in `Chapter 2`, *First Function App - Anatomy and Structure of a Function App*, the moment a photograph is uploaded into a blob container of a storage account, the Azure Function will start execution and resize the photograph and create a thumbnail of it.

The following are some of the topics that we will cover in this chapter:

- Common types of triggers
- HTTP
- Event bus
- Service bus

Common types of triggers

Let's understand first how a trigger works and get acquainted with the different types of triggers available in Azure Functions.

The architecture of a trigger and how it works is shown in the following figure:

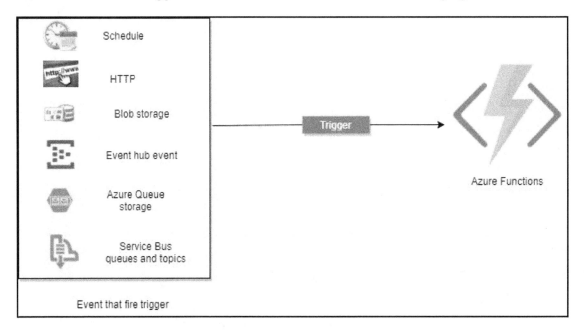

The preceding diagram shows the event that fires the trigger and once the trigger is fired, it runs the Azure Function associated with it.

We need to note a very important point here: one function must have exactly one trigger; in other words, one function can't have multiple triggers.

Now let's see the different types of trigger available in Azure:

- **TimerTrigger**: This trigger is called on a predefined schedule. We can set the time for execution of the Azure Function using this trigger.
- **BlobTrigger**: This trigger will get fired when a new or updated blob is detected. The blob contents are provided as input to the function.
- **EventHubTrigger**: This trigger is used for the application instrumentation, the user experience, workflow processing, and in the **Internet of Things** (**IoT**). This trigger will get fired when any events are delivered to an Azure event hub. We will discuss this further later in the chapter.
- **HTTPTrigger**: This trigger gets fired when the HTTP request comes. We will discuss this further later in the chapter
- **QueueTrigger**: This trigger gets fired when any new messages come in an Azure Storage queue.
- **Generic Webhook**: This trigger gets fired when the Webhook HTTP requests come from any service that supports Webhooks.
- **GitHub Webhook**: This trigger is fired when an event occurs in your GitHub repositories. The GitHub repository supports events such as Branch created, Delete branch, Issue comment, and Commit comment.
- **Service Bus trigger**: This trigger is fired when a new message comes from a service bus queue or topic.

Example of creating a simple scheduled trigger

Consider a simple example where we have to display a "good morning" message on screen every day in the morning at 8 AM. This situation is related to time so we need to use a schedule trigger. This is the type of trigger we will look at later in this chapter. Let's start creating a function with the schedule trigger first:

1. Log in to the Azure Portal.

2. Click on the top left + icon | **Compute** | **Function App**:

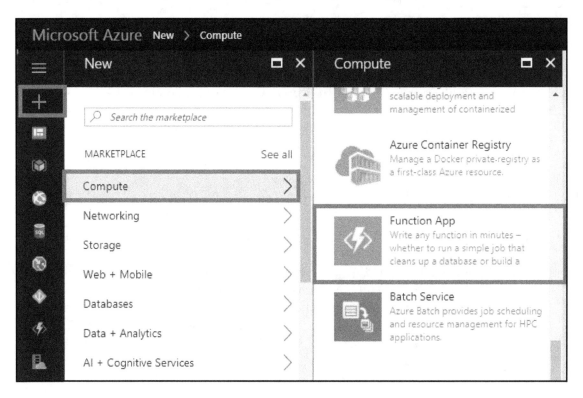

3. Once we click on **Function App,** the next screen will appear, where we have to provide a unique function **App name**, **Subscription**, **Resource Group**, **Hosting Plan**, **Location**, **Storage**, and then click on the **Create** button:

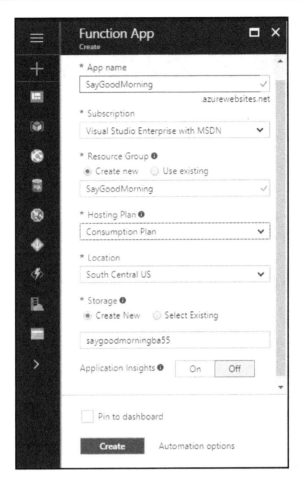

4. Once we click on the **Create** button, Azure will start to deploy this function. Once this function is deployed, it will be seen in **Notifications,** as shown in the following screenshot:

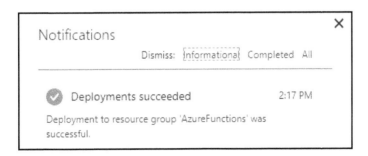

5. Click on **Notifications** and check the **Functions** details and add the trigger:

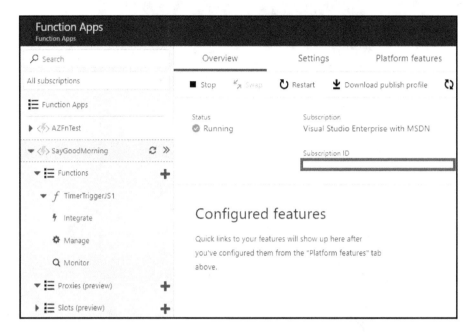

6. To add a trigger in this function, click on the **+** icon next to **Functions** and then click on **Custom function**:

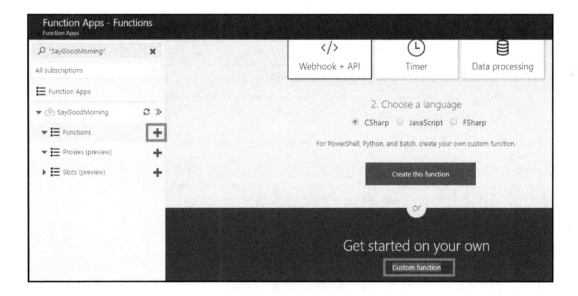

7. Now we have to select **Language** and type the name of the trigger. Once we provide the name and trigger value it will provide the available template for us after filtering all the templates:

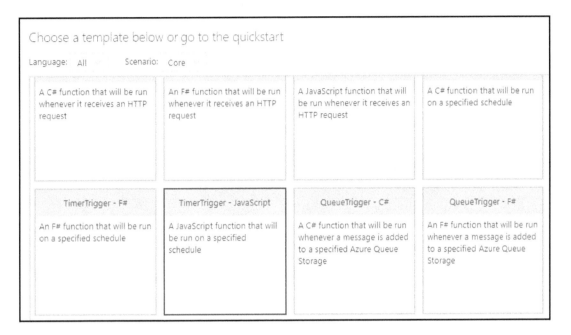

8. Scroll down and type the trigger name and schedule. The **Schedule** value is a six-field CRON expression. Click on the **Create** button:

By providing 0 0/5 * * * *, the function will run every 5 minutes from the first run.

9. Once we click on the **Create** button, we will see the template code on the screen as follows:

```
index.js        Save              ▶ Save and run
 1  module.exports = function (context, myTimer) {
 2      var timeStamp = new Date().toISOString();
 3      context.log('current time',timeStamp);
 4      if(myTimer.isPastDue)
 5      {
 6          context.log('JavaScript is running late!');
 7      }
 8      context.log('JavaScript timer trigger function ran!', timeStamp)
 9      context.log('Good Morning!!!');
10      //perform some action|
11      context.done();
12  };

Logs                          ❚❚ Pause  🗒 Clear  📋 Copy logs  ⤢ Expand  ⌄

2017-07-02T09:19:27  Welcome, you are now connected to log-streaming service.
```

Here, we have to write code. Whatever action we want to perform, we have to write it here.

Now write the code and click on the **Save and run** button.

10. Once we run the code, we can see the output in the logs, as shown in the following screenshot:

```
Logs                          ❚❚ Pause  🗒 Clear  📋 Copy logs  ⤡ Collapse  ⌄
2017-07-02T09:35:00.015 Function completed (Success, Id=2d23e1ed-00a3-4439-992e-0aa
2017-07-02T09:36:27  No new trace in the past 1 min(s).
2017-07-02T09:37:27  No new trace in the past 2 min(s).
2017-07-02T09:38:27  No new trace in the past 3 min(s).
2017-07-02T09:39:27  No new trace in the past 4 min(s).
2017-07-02T09:40:00.018 Function started (Id=336d5b04-0245-47bd-a06e-e7cfde82aee1)
2017-07-02T09:40:00.018 current time 2017-07-02T09:40:00.018Z
2017-07-02T09:40:00.018 JavaScript timer trigger function ran! 2017-07-02T09:40:00.
2017-07-02T09:40:00.018 Good Morning!!!
2017-07-02T09:40:00.018 Function completed (Success, Id=336d5b04-0245-47bd-a06e-e7c
2017-07-02T09:41:27  No new trace in the past 1 min(s).
2017-07-02T09:42:27  No new trace in the past 2 min(s).
2017-07-02T09:43:27  No new trace in the past 3 min(s).
2017-07-02T09:44:27  No new trace in the past 4 min(s).
2017-07-02T09:45:00.012 Function started (Id=abfb358e-814a-4904-ac26-e21e4764e7db)
2017-07-02T09:45:00.012 current time 2017-07-02T09:45:00.012Z
2017-07-02T09:45:00.012 JavaScript timer trigger function ran! 2017-07-02T09:45:00.
2017-07-02T09:45:00.012 Good Morning!!!
2017-07-02T09:45:00.012 Function completed (Success, Id=abfb358e-814a-4904-ac26-e21
2017-07-02T09:46:27  No new trace in the past 1 min(s).
2017-07-02T09:47:27  No new trace in the past 2 min(s).
```

Note the timing.

It runs at an interval of 5 minutes.

Now we want it to run only once a day at 8 AM. To do this, we have to change the value of the schedule.

11. To edit the value in the trigger, click on **Integrate,** type the value, and then click on the **Save** button:

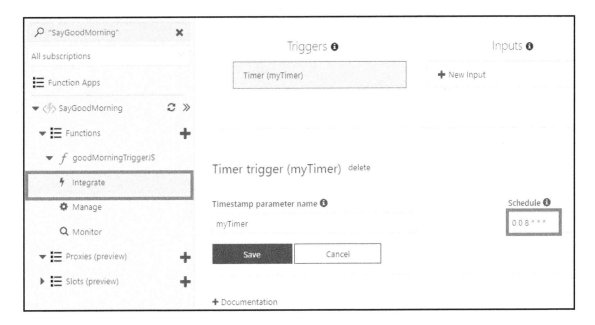

12. Now, again, click on **goodMorningTriggerJS,** modify the code, and test it.

So, this is all about creating a simple trigger with the Azure Function. Now, we will look at the different types of triggers available in Azure.

HTTP trigger

The HTTP trigger is normally used to create the API or services, where we request for data using the HTTP protocol and get the response. We can also integrate the HTTP trigger with a Webhook.

Let's start creating the HTTP trigger. We have already created a simple Azure Function and trigger. Now we will create the HTTP Login API. In this, we will send the login credential through an HTTP post request and get the response as to whether the user is valid or not.

Since we have already created a Function app in the previous example, we can now add multiple functions to it.

1. Click on + |, select **HttpTrigger-JavaScript,** provide the function name, and click on the **Create** button:

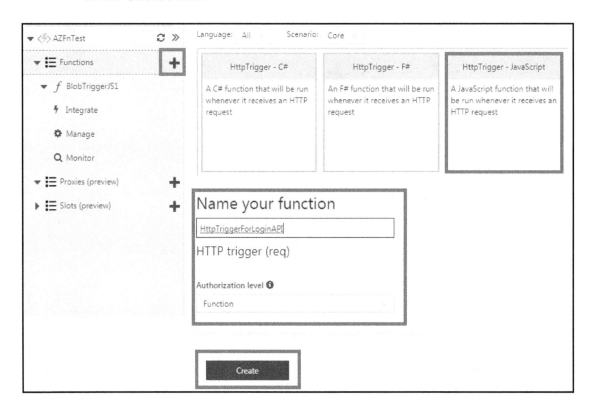

2. After we click on the **Create** button, the default template will be available. Now, we can edit and test the function:

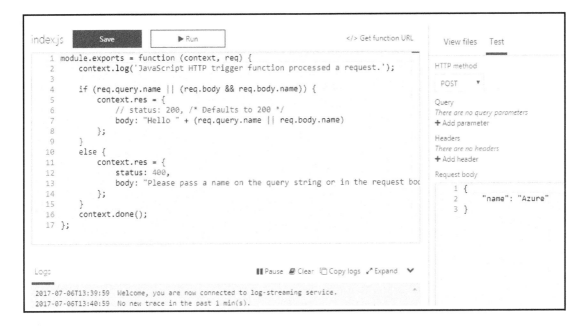

3. Now edit the code as follows:

```
module.exports = function (context, req) {
    context.log('JavaScript HTTP trigger function processed a request.');
    if (req.body && req.body.username && req.body.password) {
        if(req.body.username != 'admin' && req.body.password != '@dm!n1'){
            context.res = {
                body: "Invalid user"
            };
        }else{
            context.res = {
                body: "User" + (req.body.username)+" is valid"
            };

        }
    }
    else {
        context.res = {
            status: 400,
            body: "Please provide a username and password in the request body"
        };
    }
    context.done();
};
```

4. Save and run the code, as shown in the following screenshot:

5. The login service is ready. Now let's check this service in Postman.
6. To get the **URL** from the function, click on **Get function URL**:

7. We will use Postman to check our service. Postman is a Chrome extension for API developers to test APIs. To add the Chrome extension, go to **Settings** in Chrome and select **More tools | Extensions,** as shown in the following screenshot:

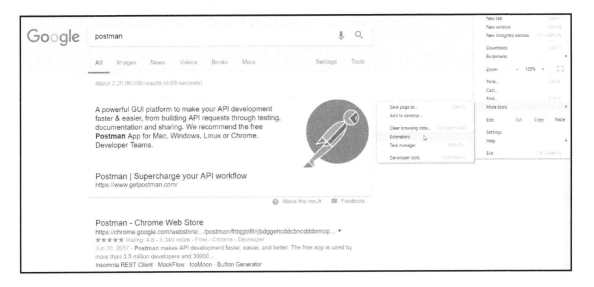

8. Click on **Get more extensions**:

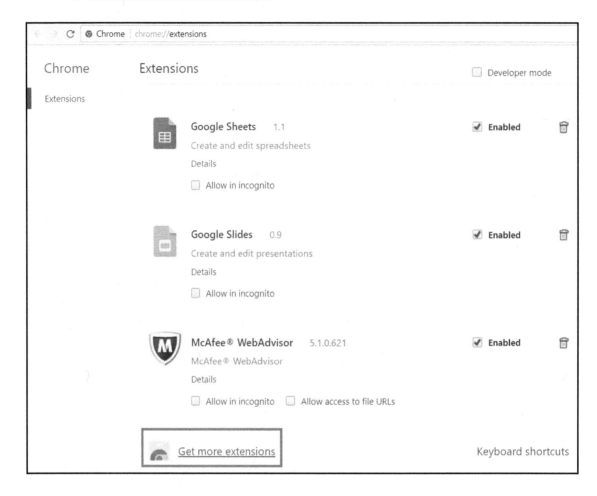

9. Now search for `postman` and then click on **+ ADD TO CHROME**:

10. Click on **Add app**:

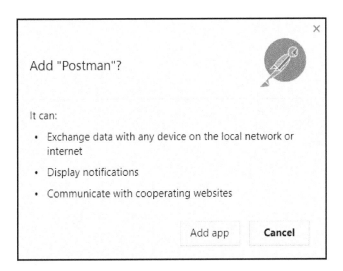

11. Launch the Postman app. Click on **Sign Up with Google**:

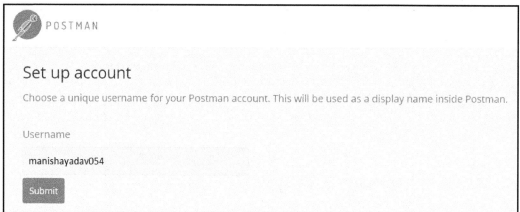

12. The Postman window will look like this:

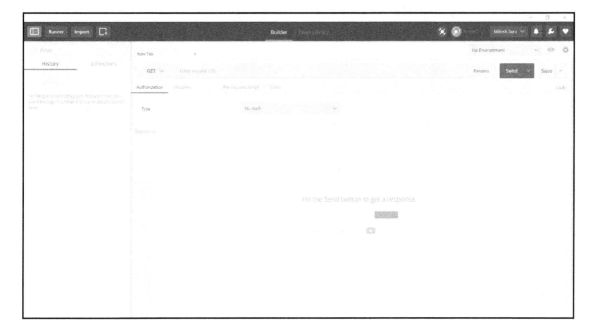

Once the initial setup is done, test the API.

13. Copy the function URL and paste it in Postman. Select the method type **POST** and provide a request body and click on the **Send** button:

>

14. If we provide the correct username and password in the request body, we will get the response, **user is valid; otherwise,** the response will be **invalid user**.

In the next section, we will discuss event hubs.

Event hubs

Event hubs are created to help us with the challenge of handling a huge amount of event-based messaging. The idea is that if we have apps or devices that publish a large amount of events in a very short duration (for example, a real-time voting system), then event hubs can be the place where we can send the event.

Event hubs will create a stream of all the events which can be processed at some point in different ways. An event hub trigger is used to respond to an event sent to an event hub event stream.

The following diagram shows how a trigger works with an **Event Hub**:

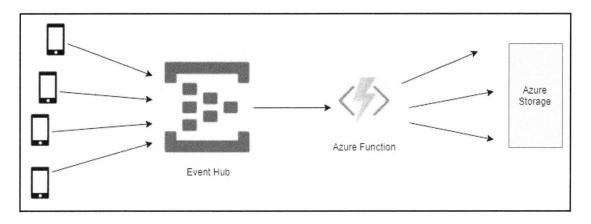

Service bus

The service bus is used to provide interaction between services or applications run in the cloud with other services or applications. The service bus trigger is used to give the response to messages which come from the service bus queue or topic.

We have two types of service bus triggers:

- **Service bus queue trigger**: A queue is basically for first-in-first-out messages. When a message comes from the service bus, the service bus queue trigger gets fired and the Azure Function is called. In the Azure Function, we can process the message and then deliver it.
- **Service bus topic trigger**: The topic is useful for scaling to very large numbers of recipients.

Summary

Finally, we have completed the trigger part of the Azure Function.

In this chapter, we have discussed the architecture of a trigger and how the trigger works. We have covered different types of triggers available in Azure.

We have created one simple example of a schedule trigger and discussed the work flow of the schedule trigger. We discussed the HTTP trigger in detail and how the HTTP trigger works. Then we created an API using the HTTP trigger. In the last section of this chapter, we covered the event hub, service bus. We also covered how a trigger works with these services.

In the next chapter, we will discuss binding, how it works with a trigger, its architecture, and other details. We will also look at some examples of triggers and binding.

4
Bindings

"Hard work beats talent when talent doesn't work hard"

– Tim Notke

The following is a list of some of the ways in which Functions can output their results:

- Available input and output bindings
- Event Bus/Service Bus
- Storage

In simple English, binding is holding things together. In the Azure Function, binding is used to bind other resources of Azure with our Azure Function.

Let's take one example where binding is required in our Azure Function. So, suppose you want to load an external configuration file from blob storage when your function starts. You need to bind the file with the Azure Function. Using binding, you do not need to hardcode anything in your code. You just need to bind the configuration file with the function and take the file from the blob storage when it starts. We can bind not only the input of the function but also the output of the function too.

So, suppose after executing the function we need to store the result in the Azure Table Storage. For that, we need our function output bind with Azure Table Storage.

A function can have multiple input and output bindings and bindings are optional.

Available input and output bindings

Bindings provide a way to connect to data for inputs and to store data for outputs, in simple terms.

Let's discuss input binding first and get familiar with it.

Types of input bindings

There are four types of input bindings:

- **Blob storage**: Blob content is used as input to the Azure Function. For example, consider a scenario where we want to create thumbnails for an image whenever a new image is uploaded to the blob storage. In this case, we will create a blob trigger with input bind and blob storage.
- **Storage tables**: Storage table content is used as input to the Azure Function. For example, instead of hardcoding configuration data in the Azure Function, store all of the configuration in the storage table and bind with the Azure Function. So when our function runs, it takes all the input from the storage table.
- **SQL tables**: SQL table data can also be used as input for the Azure Function. For example, consider a scenario where we want to check the quantity of a product at the end of every day. We have all the product details stored in the SQL table. We have the Azure Function, which is bound with the SQL table and triggers at the end of every day. Once the Azure Function runs, it takes the input from the SQL table and processes the data.
- **NoSQL DB**: No-SQL data like data, which is stored as a document, can also be used as input to the Azure Function. For example, the Azure Function reads JSON data which is stored in NoSQL DB and processes it.

In the next section, we will discuss output bindings.

Types of output bindings

There are nine types of output bindings:

- **HTTP (REST or Webhook)**: The Azure Function can produce an output as HTTP (REST or Webhook). For example, the output of the Azure Function can be linked to Webhook or can be HTTP REST.
- **Blob storage**: The Azure Function can use blob storage for output binding. For example, we have the Azure Function, which processes the image and compresses the size of image. After the image is compressed, we want it to be stored in blob storage. For this, we need output binding for the Azure Function with blob storage.
- **Events**: An event can also be bound as output from the Azure Function. We will see an example of an event as output binding to the Azure Function later in this chapter.
- **Queues and topics**: Queues and topics can also be an output from the Azure Function. We will see an example for Service Bus queues and topics as output binding to the Azure Function later in this chapter.
- **Storage tables**: Storage tables can also be bound as output to the Azure Function. Storage tables can be used as input or output to the Azure Function. For example, the Azure Function can take input from the storage table, process the data, and after processing again, store data in the storage table.
- **SQL tables**: SQL table can be used as input or output to the Azure Function. The Azure Function can read or take input from the SQL table and after processing again, can store data to the SQL table.
- **NoSQL DB**: No-SQL tables can also be used as input or output to the Azure Function. The Azure Function can read data from NoSQL DB and process it. Once the data is processed, it can be stored in NoSQL DB.
- **Push notifications**: Push notifications can be used as output binding for the Azure Function. For example, consider a scenario where we want to send a push notification with a confirmation message to all users who have registered for some marathon. For this, we will create the Azure Function and process the form of all the users and send the push notification to those users whose registration is confirmed. In this scenario, we need to use push notification as output binding to the Azure Function.

- **SendGrid email**: SendGrid email is used as output to the Azure Function. This is used when we want to send an email after execution of the Azure Function.

 So, in this section, we have given a brief overview of input and output bindings. For more details and examples, you can refer to `https://docs.` `microsoft.com/en-us/azure/azure-functions/functions-triggers-` `bindings#overview.`

In the next section, we will discuss Event Bus and Service Bus.

Types of Event Hubs

Event Hubs in Azure is a scalable data stream platform.

Event Hubs

Event Hubs are used to control traffic and capture events coming from mobile applications or web farms.

We can bind an Event Hub with the Azure Function as an trigger or output binding.

Example

We will create a Azure Function with a timer trigger and bind it with the Event Hub (output binding). Whenever a timer trigger is run in the Azure Function, an output event will be sent to the Event Hub.

The following are the steps to create an Event Hub and Azure Function:

1. Create an Event Hub in Azure.
2. Log in to the Azure Portal. Click on the plus + sign, then on **Internet of Things**, and finally on **Event Hubs** as shown in the following screenshot:

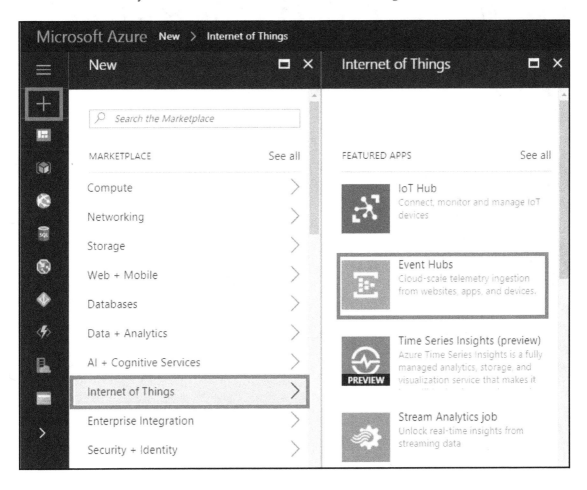

3. Provide the required details and click on **Create**:

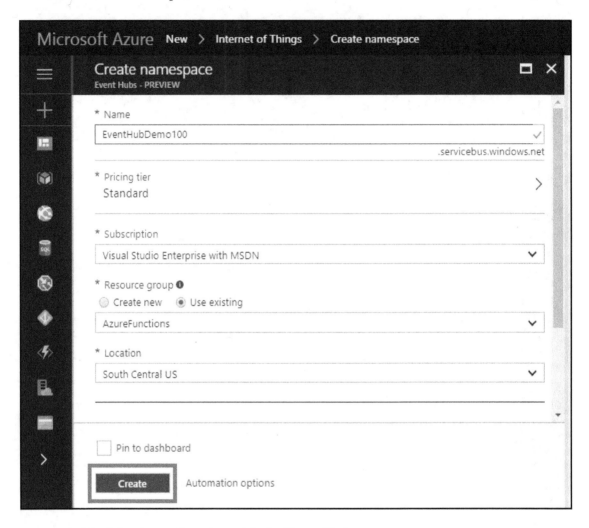

4. Bind the Azure Function with the Event Hub.

5. In the previous chapter, we created the Azure App. Now, create the Azure Function with a timer trigger, as shown in the following screenshot:

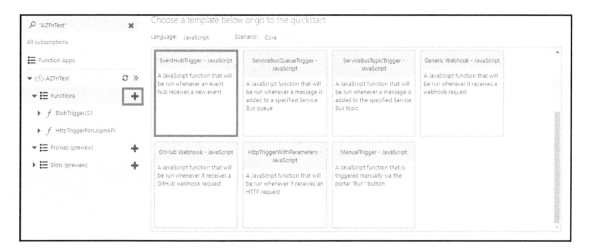

6. Provide the name and click on the **Create** button:

7. Now, configure the binding as shown in the following screenshot:

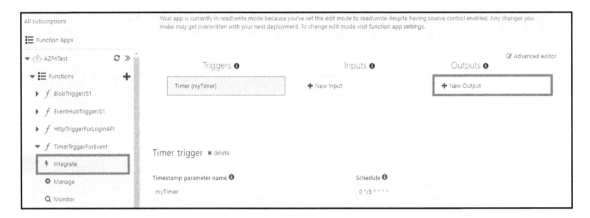

8. Select **Azure Event Hubs** and click on **Create**:

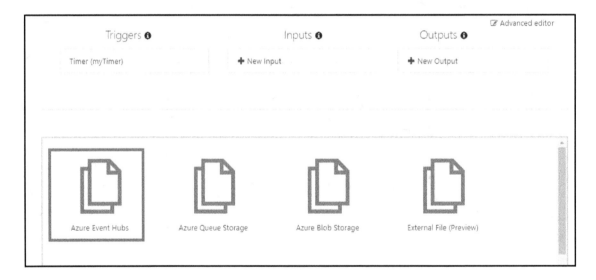

9. Now, provide the **Event parameter name**, **Event Hub name**, and **Event Hub connection**. For **Event Hub connection**, click on **new** and select the **Event Hub name**, which we created in the previous step, as shown in the following screenshot:

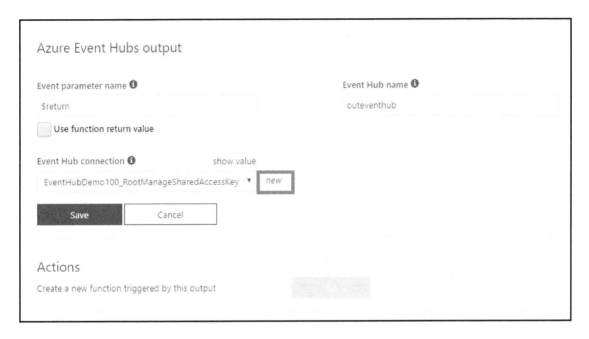

10. After clicking on **new**, you will see a pop-up, as shown in the following screenshot:

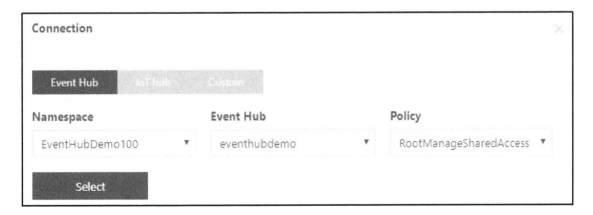

11. You will see the JSON structure after the binding is finished:

```
function.json
 1 {
 2    "bindings": [
 3      {
 4        "name": "myTimer",
 5        "type": "timerTrigger",
 6        "direction": "in",
 7        "schedule": "0 */5 * * * *"
 8      },
 9      {
10        "type": "eventHub",
11        "name": "$return",
12        "path": "outeventhub",
13        "connection": "EventHubDemo100_RootManageSharedAccessKey_EVENTHUB",
14        "direction": "out"
15      }
16    ],
17    "disabled": false
18 }
```

12. Write the code in the Azure timer trigger function, as shown in the following screenshot:

```
index.js        Save          ▶ Save and run
 1 module.exports = function (context, myTimer) {
 2     var timeStamp = new Date().toISOString();
 3     context.log('Creating Event Hub message at: ', timeStamp);
 4     context.bindings.outputEventHubMessage = "Event Hub message created at: " + timeStamp;
 5     context.done();
 6 };
```

13. Save and run the code and check the event on the Azure console, as shown in the following screenshot:

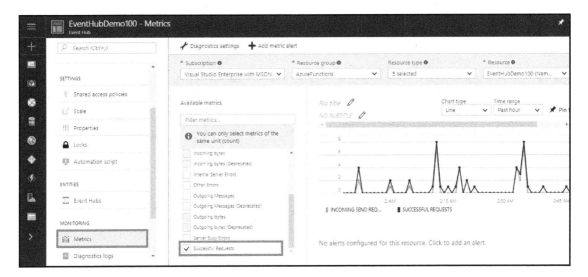

Service Bus

Service Bus is used to store queues/topics. A Service Bus queue and topic can be bound with the Azure Function.

In the previous chapter, we discussed the Service Bus queue and topic.

Now, let's see an example. We will create an Azure Function with the HTTP trigger. Whenever HTTP triggers are executed in an Azure Function, it will send a message to the queue.

1. To create a Service Bus, click on the + plus sign, then on **Enterprise Integration**, and finally on **Service Bus**:

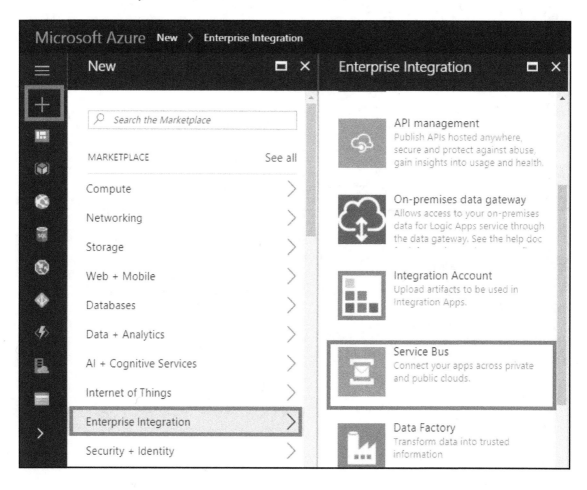

2. Now, provide all the required details and click on the **Create** button:

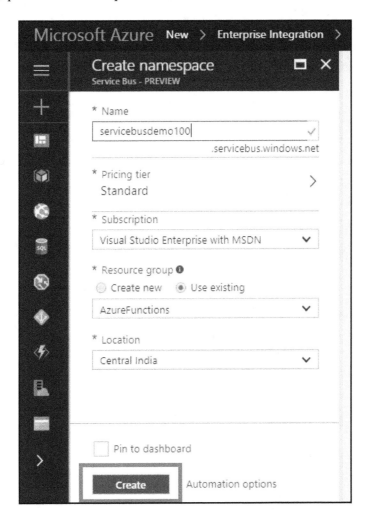

3. Now, we will create a queue. Click on **Queues** and then on **+ Queue**:

4. For queue, also provide the necessary details and click on the **Create** button:

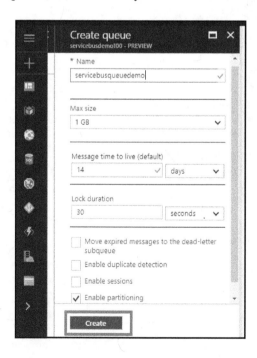

5. Create the HTTP trigger Azure Function and configure the output binding. Click on **Integrate** and then on **+ New output**:

6. Select **Azure Service Bus**, as shown in the following screenshot:

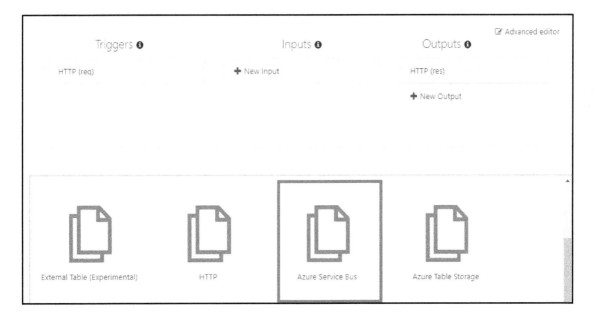

7. Configure the **Azure Service Bus**, as shown in the following screenshot:

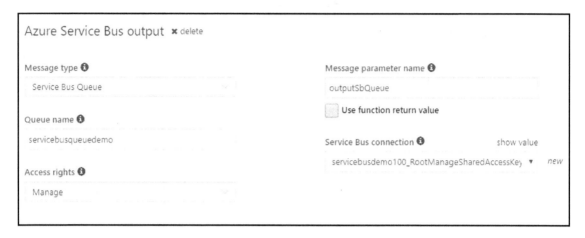

8. Once the configuration is finished, we will write code in the Azure Function, as shown in the following screenshot:

```
index.js          Save              ▶ Save and run                              </> Get function URL
 1   module.exports = function (context, req) {                                              —
 2       context.log('JavaScript HTTP trigger function processed a request.');|
 3       if (req.query.msg || (req.body && req.body.msg)) {
 4           context.res = {
 5               // status: 200, /* Defaults to 200 */
 6               body: (req.query.msg || req.body.msg)
 7           };
 8           var message = (req.query.msg || req.body.msg);
 9           context.log(message);
10           context.bindings.outputSbQueueMsg = message;
11       }
```

9. Save and run this code.
10. Now, we have successfully bound the Service Bus with our Azure Function.

Storage

Storage can be used as input or output or both as a binding for the Azure Function.

For example, consider a scenario where the Azure Function takes images as input from the blob storage and creates a thumbnail of images and saves it again in the blob storage.

In this scenario, we need blob storage to be bound as input and output.

The following are the advantages of using storage as input binding with the Azure Function:

- It allows us to take data from the storage and start processing
- Whenever data is uploaded to the storage, a trigger gets fired and the Azure Function gets executed

The following are the advantages of using storage as output binding with the Azure Function:

- It allows us to upload data to the storage after processing

Example

In this section, we will create an Azure Function with Blob storage trigger.

1. Create the Azure Function with Blob storage trigger:

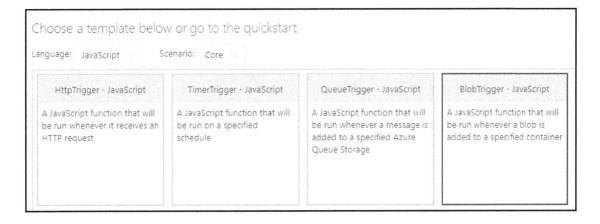

2. Configure the storage path and connection, as shown in the following screenshot:

3. Write the following code in the Azure Function:

```javascript
index.js          Save              ▶ Run

1 module.exports = function (context, myBlob) {
2     context.log("JavaScript blob trigger function processed blob");
3     context.log("Blob Name", context.bindingData.name);
4     context.log("Blob Size:", myBlob.length, "Bytes");
5     context.done();
6 };
```

4. Now, save and run the code. Once the code is run, it will show the filename and size of the file uploaded in the storage account. Upload the file in the storage account and check the log of the Azure Function.

5. Once we upload the file to the storage account, it triggers our Azure Function and we will get the filename and size of the file:

```
Logs                          ⏸ Pause  🗑 Clear  📋 Copy logs  ↗ Collapse

2017-08-15T19:53:19.099 Function started (Id=e5099c9c-1270-4bfb-9718-abb65c1cd440)
2017-08-15T19:53:19.255 JavaScript blob trigger function processed blob
2017-08-15T19:53:19.255 Blob Name download.png
2017-08-15T19:53:19.255 Blob Size: 8792 Bytes
2017-08-15T19:53:19.255 Function completed (Success, Id=e5099c9c-1270-4bfb-9718-ab
```

This was a simple example to start with storage binding.

Summary

Finally, we have reached the end of the chapter. I hope you enjoyed it !!

In this chapter, we learned binding with the Azure Function. We discussed input and output binding with the JSON structure. We have discussed the Event Hub with the Azure Function. We have created an example of binding of the Azure Function with the Event Hub. After Event Hub, we learned about Service Bus and binding of the Azure Function with the Service Bus queue. We provided simple examples for the Service Bus queue. In the last section of this chapter, we discussed storage and created one example.

In the next chapter, we will create a JavaScript function triggered by Webhook, use Webhook with Azure Functions, and use event with Azure Functions.

5

Webhooks for Azure Functions

"Simplicity is a great virtue but it requires hard work to achieve it and education to appreciate it. And to make matters worse: complexity sells better"

- Edsger Dijkstra

This chapter illustrates the use of Webhook, even binding Webhook as the output in the Azure Function. It illustrates events with simple example. We will focus on topics such as the following:

- Creating JavaScript functions triggered by Webhook
- Using a Webhook with an Azure Function
- Using an event with an Azure Function

Let's start with an introduction to Webhook before using it in our functions.

So, what is a Webhook? Webhooks are user-defined HTTP callbacks. They are usually triggered by some event, such as pushing code to a repository or a comment being posted to a blog. A web application implementing Webhooks will POST a message to a URL when certain things happen. Sometimes people call Webhooks reverse APIs, but perhaps more accurately a Webhook lets you skip a step. With most APIs, there's a request followed by a response. No request is required for a Webhook, it just sends the data when it's available.

Let's start with a simple example.

Creating a JavaScript function triggered by a Webhook

Let's create a JavaScript function in Microsoft Azure using Azure Portal:

1. Log in to the Azure portal and navigate to the function app, which we created in the previous chapter.

2. Click on the + sign to add a new Azure Function. Set the language as **Javascript** and the template as **Generic Webhook**, as shown in the following screenshot:

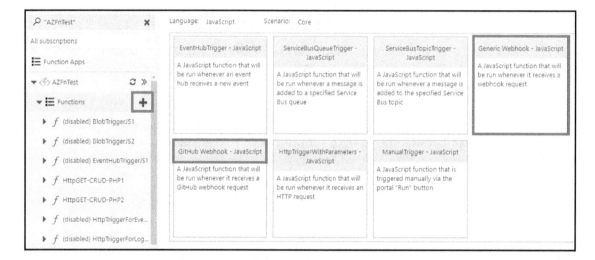

3. Now provide a name for the function and click on **Create**:

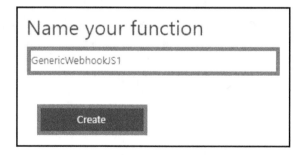

4. A default template will be created, as shown in the following screenshot:

```
index.js          Save              ▶ Run                                              </>

 1  module.exports = function (context, data) {
 2      context.log('Webhook was triggered!');
 3
 4      // Check if we got first/last properties
 5      if('first' in data && 'last' in data) {
 6          context.res = {
 7              body: { greeting: 'Hello ' + data.first + ' ' + data.last + '!'}
 8          };
 9      }
10      else {
11          context.res = {
12              status: 400,
13              body: { error: 'Please pass first/last properties in the input object'}
14          };
15      }
16
17      context.done();
18  }
19
```

5. Get the function URL and copy it. We will use it later in the chapter. Save it in a notepad:

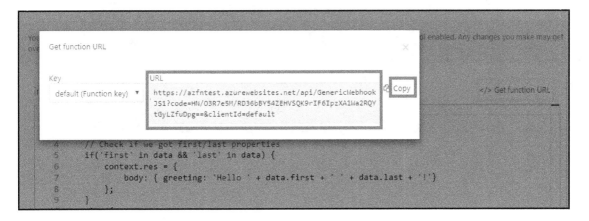

6. Now, we will create a Webhook endpoint in an activity log alert in Azure Monitor. Click on **Monitor**, as shown in the following screenshot:

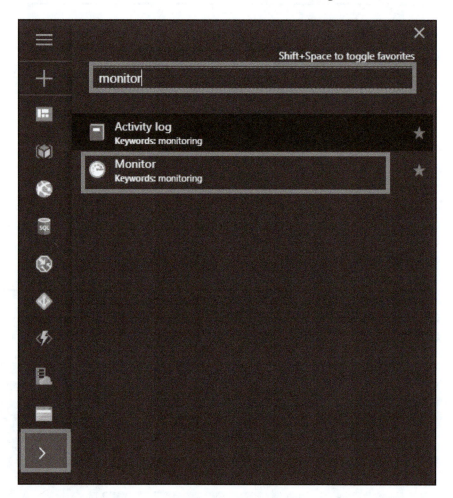

7. Now we need to create an alert. Click on **Alerts** and then on **Add activity log alert**:

8. Provide the following details:

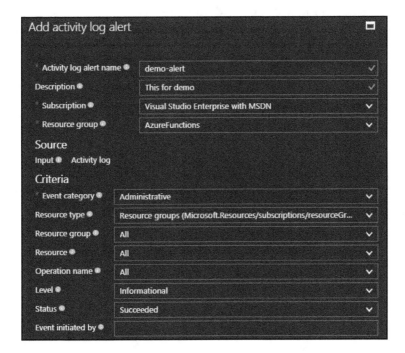

9. Here's a description of the terms in the preceding screenshot:
    - * **Activity log alert name**: Name of the activity log alert.
    - * **Subscription**: Microsoft Azure subscription.
    - * **Resource group**: This is the resource group that the alert resources are deployed to. Using the same resource group as your function app makes it easier to clean up after you have finished, and it also helps when we want to assign role-based access to resources.
    - * **Event category**: This includes changes made to Azure resources.
    - * **Resource type**: This filters alerts to resource group activities.
    - * **Resource group**: This monitors all resources.
    - * **Operation name**: This filters alerts to create operations, for example, Get Resource Group, Create Resource Group, Delete Resource Group, Move Resource Group, and Validate Move Resource Group.
    - * **Level**: This includes informational-level alerts, for example, Information, Warning, and Error.
    - * **Status**: This filters alerts to actions that have completed successfully, for example, the resource group status will be Failed, Started, or Succeeded.
    - In criteria, we need to define the alert criteria. Since we are creating an alert on the resource group, we need to set the **Resource type** to **Resource groups**.

10. Now scroll down and specify the **Actions** for the alert, as shown in the following screenshot:

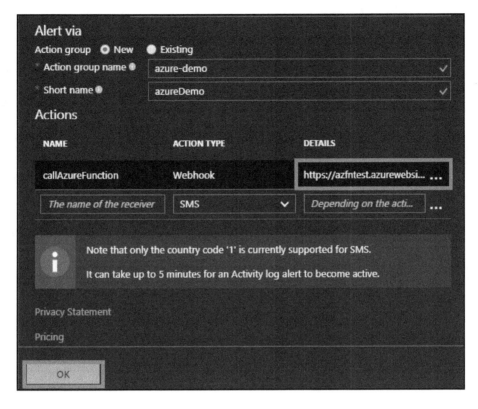

11. In **Alert via**, provide the following details:

- * **Action group**: This creates a new action group, which defines the action to be taken when an alert is raised
- * **Action group name**: This is the name to identify the action group with
- * **Short name**: This is a short name for the action group

12. In **Actions**, provide the following details:

- **NAME**: This is the name of the action
- **ACTION TYPE**: This is the response to the alert that a Webhook URL is called
- **DETAILS**: You need to paste this in the Webhook URL of the function that you copied earlier

13. Once the alert is created, it will be seen in the Monitor list, as shown in the following screenshot:

14. Now, once again go to your Azure Function and modify the code as shown in the following screenshot:

```
index.js        Save              ▶ Save and run

 1  module.exports = function (context, data) {
 2  |   context.log('Webhook was triggered!');
 3      var obj = data.data;
 4      if(obj) {
 5          context.log(obj.context);
 6          context.res = {
 7              body: {data:'data'+ obj.context}
 8          };
 9      }
10      else {
11          context.res = {
12              status: 400,
13              body: { error: 'Please pass input object'}
14          };
15      }
16      context.done();
17  }
```

15. Now, click on the **Save and run** button and see the log. The **Logs** will look like the following screenshot:

16. Now we will test our Azure Function by adding new resource group. Navigate to **Resource groups** and click on the **+ Add** button, as shown in the following screenshot:

17. Provide the **Resource group name**, **Resource group location**, and **Subscription** for the **Resource group** and click on the **Create** button to create the **Resource group**:

18. Once the **Resource group** is created, go to the Azure Function that we have created and check the logs. The activity log alert triggers the Webhook and the function executes:

```
Logs                                          ▮▮ Pause  🗑 Clear  🗐 Copy logs  ↗ Collapse  ⌄

2017-09-03T10:19:07.521 Function started (Id=e9a0be59-bbef-4337-88ab-87b5e628d28d)
2017-09-03T10:19:07.521 Webhook was triggered!
2017-09-03T10:19:07.521 Function completed (Success, Id=e9a0be59-bbef-4337-88ab-87b5e628d28d, Duration=1ms)
2017-09-03T10:20:56  No new trace in the past 1 min(s).
2017-09-03T10:21:22.955 Function started (Id=a63a5bba-a50d-499c-b0e0-53acf5586c71)
2017-09-03T10:21:22.955 Webhook was triggered!
2017-09-03T10:21:22.976 { activityLog:
  { authorization:
    { action: 'Microsoft.Resources/subscriptions/resourcegroups/write',
      scope: '/subscriptions/                                  resourcegroups/testingWebhook' },
    channels: 'Operation',
    claims: '{"aud":"https://management.core.windows.net/","iss":"https://sts.windows.net/b76e984d-14f8-48b9-940c-dceca5c4
    caller:
    correlationId: '28724c23-4852-4983-b8b3-57364a41f82e',
    description: '',
    eventSource: 'Administrative',
    eventTimestamp: 2017-09-03T10:20:52.233Z,
    httpRequest: '{"clientRequestId":"d2ac0b41-e661-4db3-b9c3-5402944790dc","clientIpAddress":"103.57.173.255","method":"F ⌄
```

19. Look at the `activityLog` object in the **Logs** window. It gives all the details related to the resource group. You can see the **resourceGroupName**, which we have created for testing, with the **status** as **Succeeded**, and the **subStatus** as **Created**:

```
Logs                                           ❚❚ Pause  🗑 Clear  📋 Copy logs  ↗ Collapse  ⌄

    httpRequest: '{"clientRequestId":"d2ac0b41-e661-4db3-b9c3-5402944790dc","clientIpAddress":"103.57.173.255","method":"P▲
    eventDataId: 'cc07e943-8eb6-47b6-8202-66740cc28f99',
    level: 'Informational',
    operationName: 'Microsoft.Resources/subscriptions/resourcegroups/write',
    operationId: '28724c23-4852-4983-b8b3-57364a41f82e',
    properties:
    { statusCode: 'Created',
      serviceRequestId: null,
      responseBody: '{"id":"/subscriptions/b88f4447-ad0e-44d4-a662-2eb5c950f091/resourceGroups/testingWebhook","name":"te
    resourceId: '/subscriptions/                              resourcegroups/testingWebhook',
    resourceGroupName: 'testingWebhook',
    resourceProviderName: 'Microsoft.Resources',
    status: 'Succeeded',
    subStatus: 'Created',
    subscriptionId:
    submissionTimestamp: 2017-09-03T10:21:10.338Z,
    resourceType: 'Microsoft.Resources/subscriptions/resourcegroups' } }
2017-09-03T10:21:22.976 Function completed (Success, Id=a63a5bba-a50d-499c-b0e0-53acf5586c71, Duration=8ms)
```

20. Now we have completed the example. It's always a good practice to delete resources that are no longer in use. So, delete the resource group that we have created for testing.
21. To delete the resource group, navigate to **Resource group** and click on the **Resource group name**, and then on the **Delete** button.

Using a Webhook with an Azure Function

We have already seen how to trigger an Azure Function with as Webhook. We can also trigger a Webhook with our Azure Function. We can bind the Webhook as an input to our Azure Function.

To bind a Webhook as an input to our Azure Function, create an HTTP trigger in the Azure Function:

1. Click on + sign to add the Azure Function and select **HttpTrigger - JavaScript**, as shown in the following screenshot:

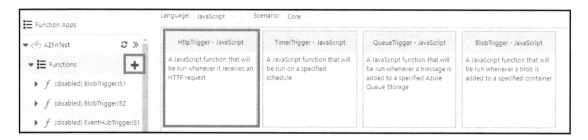

2. Provide a name for the function and click on the **Create** button.
3. Once the **HttpTrigger** is created, click on the **Integrate** button, as shown in the following screenshot:

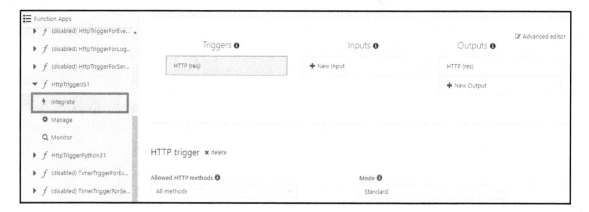

4. Now, check the options and change the **Mode** to **Webhook**. There will be only two options available: the first is **Standard** and the second is **Webhook**. By default, the **Standard** mode is selected.

5. Once we change the **Mode** to **Webhook**, we will see another option, **Webhook type**.

6. Three types of Webhook are available in the Azure Function:

   - * **GitHub**
   - * **Generic JSON**
   - * **Slack**

7. Depending on our needs, we can select any of these, as shown in the following screenshot:

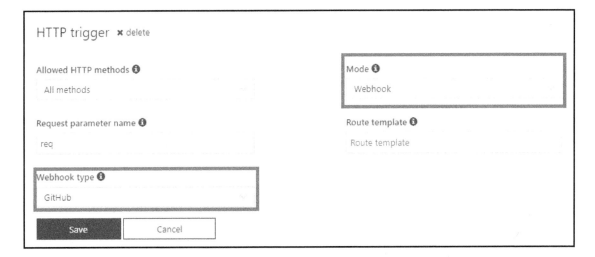

8. Click on the **Save** button to save the changes.

9. Now, check `function.json` and observe the changes, as shown in the following screenshot:

```
function.json    Save         ▶        </> Get function   </> Get GitHub      View files   Test
                              Run       URL                secret

1  {                                                                          ＋ Add    ⬆ Upload    🗑 Delete
2    "bindings": [
3      {                                                                      📂 HttpTriggerJS1
4        "type": "httpTrigger",
5        "direction": "in",                                                     📄 function.json
6        "name": "req",
7        "webHookType": "github"                                               📄 index.js
8      },
9      {
10       "type": "http",
11       "direction": "out",
12       "name": "res"
13     }
14   ],
15   "disabled": false
16 }
```

10. In this way, we can bind a Webhook with our Azure Function.

Using an event with an Azure Function

Events are things that trigger our Azure Functions to run. Events can be HTTP endpoints, message queues, blob updates, and cron-scheduled events. To elaborate more by giving an example, what if you want to be notified when a file is uploaded on blob storage or you want to immediately process a file when it is uploaded to blob storage?

The following diagram shows how the Azure Function works, which gets triggered when an event occurs:

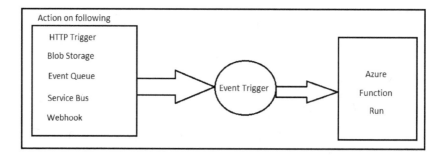

The following are the types of event that cause the function to run:

- **HTTP Trigger**: This is an event that causes the function to run whenever it receives an HTTP request.
- **Timer Trigger**: This type of trigger is run on the basis of a schedule. We can set the time for the trigger and the function runs at that specified time.
- **Queue Trigger**: The Azure Function will run whenever a message is added to a specified Azure queue storage.
- **Blob Trigger**: The Azure Function will run whenever a blob is added to a specified container, for example, uploading an image in storage.
- **EventHub Trigger**: The Azure Function will run whenever an event hub receives a new event.
- **ServiceBus Queue Trigger**: In this case, the Azure Function will be triggered whenever a message is added to a specified service bus queue.
- **ServiceBus Topic Trigger**: This is same as the ServiceBus Queue Trigger. The Azure Function will be triggered whenever a topic is added to a specified service bus topic.
- **Generic Webhook Trigger**: In this case, the Azure Function runs whenever it receives a Webhook request.
- **GitHub Webhook Trigger**: This trigger runs the Azure Function whenever it receives a GitHub Webhook request, for example, commit, create branch, push, or pull code from GitHub. GitHub has the option to create a Webhook for a particular action performed on GitHub.

Summary

Finally, we have reached the end of the chapter. In this chapter, we learned about Webhooks. We discussed the introduction of Webhooks and how they are different from APIs. We have created a JavaScript function triggered by a Webhook, which gets triggered when the new resource group is added to Azure. We created an activity alert in Azure monitor for a Webhook and bound it to our Azure Function.

Then, we tested our function by creating resource groups. Further, we saw how to bind the Webhook to our Azure Function. We bound it as an output to our HTTP trigger. In the last section of this chapter, we discussed events in relation to Azure Functions.

In the next chapter, we will do some exercise that will use all the concepts we have explained so far and create a real-life example. We will give an outline of the project, the solution, and its implementation as well.

6

The Real World - Functions to Build Consumable APIs

"Elegance is not a dispensable luxury but a factor that decides between success and failure"

– Edsger Dijkstra

In this chapter, we will show how the previous concepts of triggers and bindings work together to bring some real-world functionality.

In the previous chapter, we have learned about triggers and bindings and how they work. In this chapter, we will do some exercises, which will use all the previous concepts, and create real-life examples:

- Outlining a project
- Architecting the solution
- Building a project
- Using storage
- Testing

Outlining a project

Let's start with the project's outline. We are going to create a User Detail Portal.

This portal will be used by the client for their users, who can enter their details, which will be stored in the database.

Once the data is stored in the database, the client can use that data anytime in the future.

The detailed process is where we will create one form for the user, which will take the ID, name, age, and address as parameters and save all the data in the database.

To create this, we first need to create APIs using the HTTP trigger of the Azure Function. After that, we will create a form using HTML, CSS, and JavaScript.

Architecting the solution

The following diagram shows the solution's architecture:

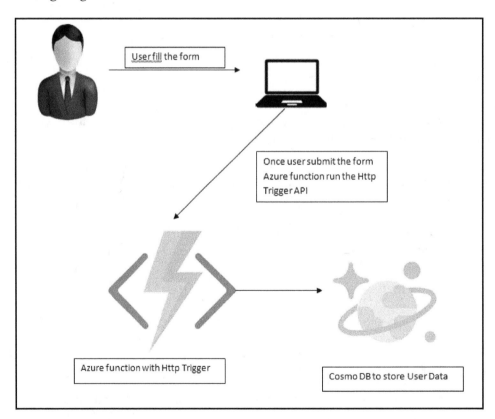

As we discussed at the start of the chapter, the user will fill in the form and submit the data. Once the data gets submitted, the HTTP trigger of the Azure Function processes the request and puts the data in the database.

In the preceding architecture diagram, the user will fill all the details in the form. Once the user submits the form, `HttpRequest` will be sent to Azure Function and `HttpTrigger` gets fired. `HttpTrigger` executes the code, which stores user details in Cosmos DB.

Now, in the next section, we will start our project.

Building the project

Now, we will start to build our project. First we will create the API for storing data in Cosmos DB. Once the API is created, we will then move on to design our user form using HTML and CSS.

For creating APIs, we need to create `HttpTrigger` in Azure Function.

Let's start with the creation of the API using Azure Function:

1. First, login to the Azure portal. Navigate to the Function App, which we have created in the previous chapter.
2. Click on the plus sign, select the language as **JavaScript**, and click on the `HttpTrigger` function, as shown in the following screenshot:

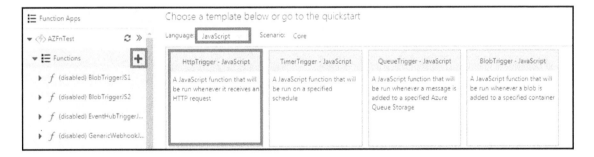

3. Now, provide a name to the function and click on **Create**:

4. Once the function is created, the default code will be opened:

```
index.js        Save            ▶ Run                                          </> Get function URL

 1  module.exports = function (context, req) {
 2      context.log('JavaScript HTTP trigger function processed a request.');
 3
 4      if (req.query.name || (req.body && req.body.name)) {
 5          context.res = {
 6              // status: 200, /* Defaults to 200 */
 7              body: "Hello " + (req.query.name || req.body.name)
 8          };
 9      }
10      else {
11          context.res = {
12              status: 400,
13              body: "Please pass a name on the query string or in the request body
14          };
15      }
16      context.done();
17  };
```

5. Now, we need to create the API, which takes an input from the request and stores the output in the database. So, click on **Integrate** to add output binding:

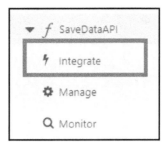

6. Now, click on **Outputs** to add output binding as Cosmos DB:

7. Select **Azure Cosmos DB**, and then click on the **Select** button:

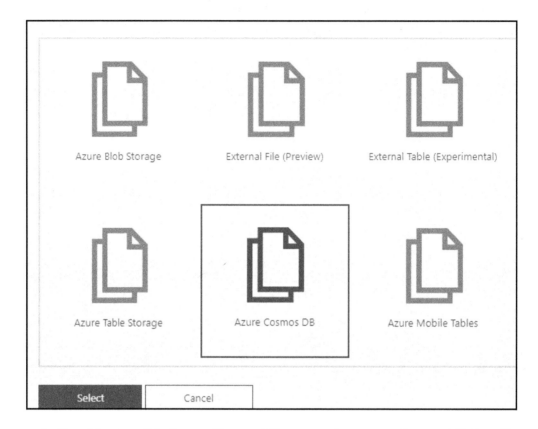

8. To add output binding as Cosmos DB, we need to create Cosmos DB first. To create Cosmos DB, click on **new**:

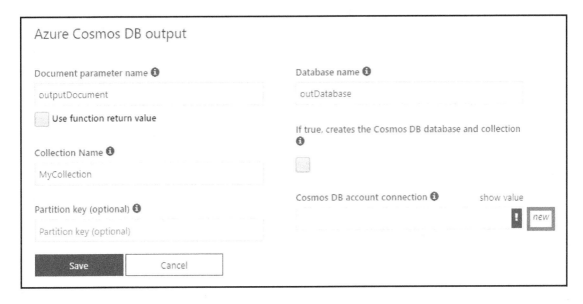

9. Now, provide all the details in the form for creating Azure Cosmos DB, and click on the **OK** button, as shown in the following screenshot:

10. Once Azure Cosmos DB is created, select it in **Cosmo DB account connection**, as shown in the following screenshot:

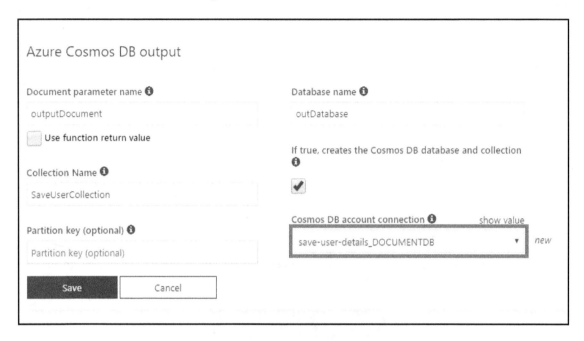

11. Now, look at the `function.json` file:

```
11          "direction": "out",
12          "name": "res"
13      },
14      {
15          "type": "documentDB",
16          "name": "outputDocument",
17          "databaseName": "Users",
18          "collectionName": "UserDataCollection",
19          "createIfNotExists": true,
20          "connection": "save-user-details_DOCUMENTDB",
21          "direction": "out"
22      }
23      ],
24      "disabled": false
25  }
```

Examine the JSON format of the `function.json` file. It contains all the details of binding with Azure Cosmos DB.

12. Open the `index.json` file and write the following code:

```
module.exports = function (context, req) {
    context.log('JavaScript HTTP trigger function processed a request.');
    if (req.body && req.body.name && req.body.id && req.body.age && req.body.address) {

        context.res = {
            // status: 200, /* Defaults to 200 */
            body: "Data is saved for user " + (req.body.name) +" !!"
        };

        context.bindings.outputDocument = JSON.stringify({
        id: req.body.id,
        name: req.body.name,
        age: req.body.age,
        address: req.body.address
        });
    }
    else {
        context.res = {
            status: 400,
            body: "Please pass all user details"
        };
    }
    context.done();
};
```

In the preceding code, we are taking the user details and binding them with our `outputDocument`. Once we bind it with `outputDocument`, it will enter the details in the Azure Cosmos DB.

13. Now we have created our API. Let's test it. Go to the **Test** tab, provide the JSON, and click on the **Run** button, as shown in the following screenshot:

```
index.js        Save            ▶         </> Get function       View files   Test
                                Run        URL
                                                                  Request body
 1  module.exports = function (context, req) {                     1
 2      context.log('JavaScript HTTP trigger function pro          2    "id":"1",|
 3      if (req.body && req.body.name && req.body.id && r          3    "name": "Manisha",
 4                                                                 4    "age":"24",
 5          context.res = {                                        5    "address":"Mumbai"
 6              // status: 200, /* Defaults to 200 */              6
 7              body: "Data is saved for user " + (req.bo
 8          };
 9
10          context.bindings.outputDocument = JSON.strin
11          id: req.body.id,
12          name: req.body.name,
13          age: req.body.age,
14          address: req.body.address
15          });
```

14. You can see the response in the following screenshot:

```
Output                    ✔ Status: 200 OK

"Data is saved for user Manisha
```

15. Now we will check our entry in Cosmos DB. Navigate to **Azure Cosmos DB**. Click on **More services**, type **Cosmo**, and then select **Azure Cosmos DB**, as shown in the following screenshot:

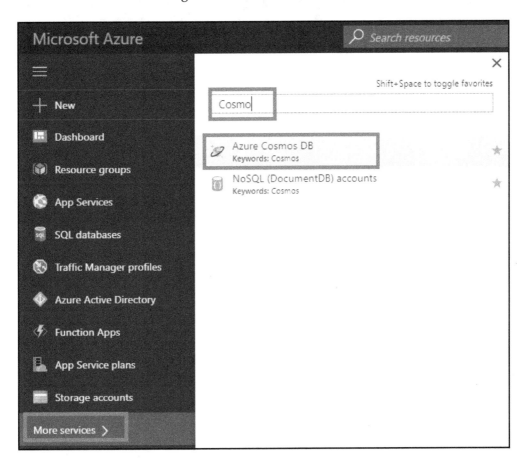

16. Click on **save-user-details** as shown in the following screenshot:

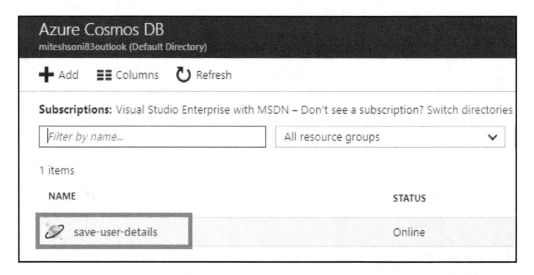

17. Now, from the list of options click on **Data Explorer (Preview)**. We will see our **Users** database:

18. Click on the **Users** database and then click on **Documents**:

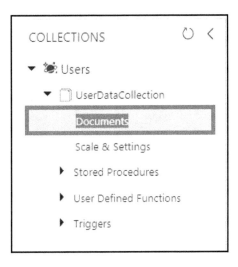

19. Now, see our entry; it should be there in the list, as shown in the following screenshot:

```
1  {
2      "id": "1",
3      "name": "Manisha",
4      "age": "24",
5      "address": "Mumbai",
6      "_rid": "U+0pAKrjdAABAAAAAAAAAA==",
7      "_self": "dbs/U+0pAA==/colls/U+0pAKrjdAA=/docs/U+0pAKrjdAAB
8      "_etag": "\"00000309-0000-0000-0000-59b1a6eb0000\"",
9      "_attachments": "attachments/",
10     "_ts": 1504814827
11  }
```

20. If the entry are coming to databases, it means that our API is working as expected.

21. Now, copy the URL and save it for future use. Click on **</> Get function URL**:

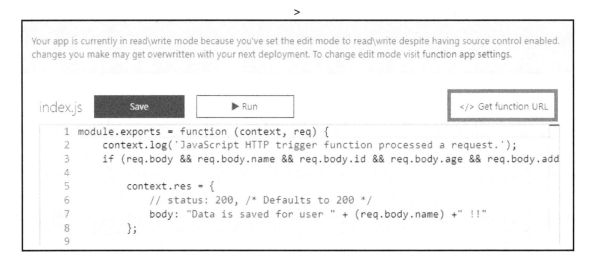

22. You will get a popup from there; click on **Copy**. Now, the URL is copied; save it somewhere as shown in the following screenshot:

23. Now, the API is created. Let's create our portal. We have used NetBeans 8.1 to create it.

24. Open NetBeans and create a new **Java Web** project:

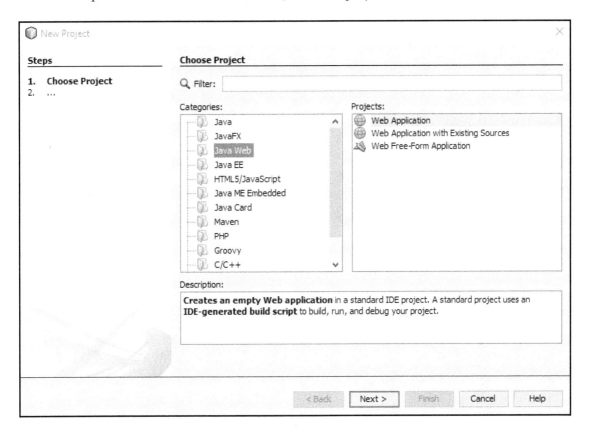

25. Click on **Next**:

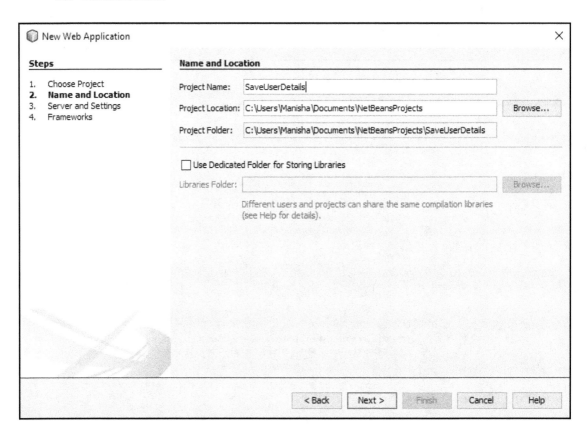

26. Give a name to the project and click on **Next**:

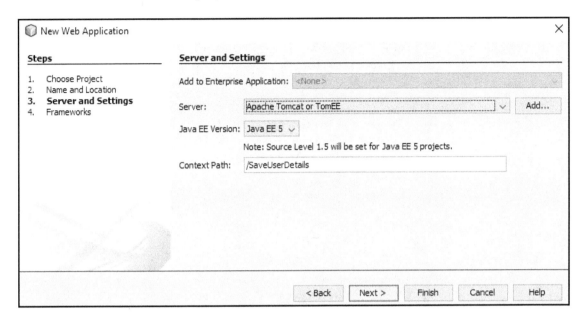

27. Now, click on **Finish** to create the web project.

28. The default structure of the project is shown as follows:

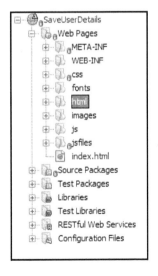

29. Now, in the `index.html` file, write the following code:

```html
<html>
    <head>
        <title>Add User Details</title>
        <meta charset="UTF-8">
        <meta name="application-name" content="User Details">
        <meta content="initial-scale=1.0, width=device-width"
name="viewport">
        <link rel="stylesheet" href="css/bootstrap.min.css"/>
        <link rel="stylesheet" href="css/user.css"/>
    </head>
    <body>
        <div class="start">
            <div class="header">
                <div class="text-center">User Details
Form</div>
            </div>
            <div class="login">
            <form class="form-horizontal" autocomplete="off"
name="userForm" id="userForm">
                <div class="form-group">
                    <div class="col-sm-12">
                        Id:<input type="text" class="form-
control marginAuto" id="userId" placeholder="Id" required
autofocus>
                    </div>
                </div>
                <div class="form-group">
                    <div class="col-sm-12">
                        Name:<input type="text" class="form-
control marginAuto"  id="username" placeholder="Username"
required >
                    </div>
                </div>
                <div class="form-group">
                    <div class="col-sm-12">
                        Age:<input type="text" class="form-
control marginAuto"  id="userAge" placeholder="Age" required>
                    </div>
                </div>
                <div class="form-group">
                    <div class="col-sm-12">
                        Address:<input type="text" class="form-
control marginAuto"  id="userAddress" placeholder="Address"
required>
                    </div>
                </div>
```

```
                     <div class="form-group">
                         <div class="col-sm-12">
                             <div id="submitDiv">
                                 <button id="submit" name="submit"
        type="submit" class="btn btn-default" ng-
        click="validate()">Submit</button>
                             </div>
                         </div>
                     </div>
                 </form>
            </div>
                <div class="footer"><div>Footer goes
        here...</div></div>
            </div>
            <script src="js/jquery-1.11.3.min.js"></script>
            <script src="js/jquery-ui.min.js"></script>
            <script src="js/bootstrap.min.js"></script>
            <script src="jsfiles/user.js"></script>
        </body>
    </html>
```

Now, let's understand the code first. This is an **HTML (Hyper Text Markup Language)** file. HTML is the standard markup language for creating web pages. HTML describes the structure of web pages using markup. HTML elements are the building blocks of HTML pages. HTML elements are represented by tags.

The parent tag of this file is the <html> tag. All the content will come under this tag only:

```
<head>
        <title>Add User Details</title>
        <meta charset="UTF-8">
        <meta name="application-name" content="User Details">
        <meta content="initial-scale=1.0, width=device-width"
name="viewport">
        <link rel="stylesheet" href="css/bootstrap.min.css"/>
        <link rel="stylesheet" href="css/user.css"/>
</head>
```

This <head> tag includes the title of the page, metadata for the page, and the link to the stylesheet.

The main contain of the page is start in <body> tag.

Inside the `<body>` tag, we will create our form and a heading for the form:

```
<div class="header">
            <div class="text-center">User Details Form</div>
        </div>
This is an heading for the form.

        <form class="form-horizontal" autocomplete="off"
name="userForm" id="userForm">
            <div class="form-group">
                <div class="col-sm-12">
                    Id:<input type="text" class="form-control
marginAuto" id="userId" placeholder="Id" required autofocus>
                </div>
            </div>
            <div class="form-group">
                <div class="col-sm-12">
                    Name:<input type="text" class="form-control
marginAuto"  id="username" placeholder="Username" required >
                </div>
            </div>
            <div class="form-group">
                <div class="col-sm-12">
                    Age:<input type="text" class="form-control
marginAuto"  id="userAge" placeholder="Age" required>
                </div>
            </div>
            <div class="form-group">
                <div class="col-sm-12">
                    Address:<input type="text" class="form-control
marginAuto"  id="userAddress" placeholder="Address" required>
                </div>
            </div>
            <div class="form-group">
                <div class="col-sm-12">
                    <div id="submitDiv">
                        <button id="submit" name="submit" type="submit"
class="btn btn-default" ng-click="validate()">Submit</button>
                    </div>
                </div>
            </div>
        </form>
```

Our form design will start with the `<form>` tag and end with the `</form>` tag, as shown in the preceding code.

In the end of the file, we have the code for the page footer:

```
<div class="footer"><div>Footer goes here...</div></div>
```

Now, we need to write the reference to the JavaScript file:

```
<script src="js/jquery-1.11.3.min.js"></script>
<script src="js/jquery-ui.min.js"></script>
<script src="js/bootstrap.min.js"></script>
```

These three JavaScript files are external open source .js files. We can directly download and include them in our project:

```
<script src="jsfiles/user.js"></script>
```

This is a user-defined JavaScript file. In this file, we will write what action we need to perform once the user submits the form:

1. For styling, we need to create the .css file. We can create any design we want by modifying the .css file. Create the .css file inside the css folder, and write the following code:

```
.start{
    /* position: absolute; */
    top: 0px;
    /* margin-left: 0; */
    /* margin-top: 0; */
    padding-left: 0;
    z-index: 10;
    width: 860px;
    height: 636px;
    background-color: #FFFFFF;
    left: 0;
    margin: 0 auto;
    box-shadow: 0px 2px 6px rgba(0, 0, 0, 0.5);
}
.header{
    height:115px;
    /*background-image: url("../images/background-
header.png");*/
    box-shadow: 0px 2px 6px rgba(0, 0, 0, 0.5);
    background-color: green;
}
.left-header{
    padding-top:42px;
    padding-left: 10px;
    float: left;
```

```css
    font-size: 22px;
    color:#FFFFFF;
}
.right-header{
    padding-top:42px;
    padding-left: 68%;
    float: left;
}
.footer {
    position: fixed;
    bottom: 0%;
    left: 50%;
    width: 860px;
    height: 28px;
    margin-left: -430px;/*Half of Width*/
    background-color: green;
    clear: both;
    box-shadow: 0px 2px 6px rgba(0, 0, 0, 0.5);
    text-align: center;
    font-size: 14px;
    color:#ffffff;
    /*font-weight: bold;*/
}
.login{
    width: 300px;
    margin-left: 280px;
    margin-top: 110px;

}
.marginAuto{
    margin-left: auto;
    margin-right: auto;
}

#submitDiv>button{
    width:300px;
    background-color: green;
    color:#ffffff;
        /*margin-left: 10px;*/
}
.headerOptions{
    display: none;
}
.text-center{
    text-align: center;
    font-size: 20px;
    color: #fff;
    padding-top: 46px;
```

```
}
```

This is a **CSS (Cascading Style Sheet)** file. CSS is a language that describes the style of an HTML page. CSS describes how HTML elements should be displayed on web pages. For example, assign the background color, font color, width, and height to a particular element in the HTML file. We can assign the same property to multiple elements in the HTML file by defining a class in the CSS file.

In the CSS file, we can create classes and IDs for the HTML element.

The class is created if we want to apply the same property to multiple elements. The ID is used for unique elements in the HTML file.

CSS is very simple and make it easy to modify the design of HTML web pages.

2. Now, we need to create the user.js file in the .js file folder. In this, we have the Ajax call, where we need to paste our Azure Function URL. Write the following code:

```javascript
$(document).ready(function() {
    $("#userForm").submit(function(event){
        if($("#userId").val() && $("#username").val()){
            var id = $("#userId").val();
            var username = $("#username").val();
            var age = $("#userAge").val();
            var address = $("#userAddress").val();
            var userJSON = JSON.stringify({
                "id":id,
                "name":username,
                "age":age,
                "address":address
            });
            $.ajax({
                type: "POST",
                contentType: "application/json",
url:'https://azfntest.azurewebsites.net/api/SaveDataAPI?code=YP
hjNyIo4gX2X5F6Nlv/6uwuKOrszcJHpRAuQeE9AzaODOA0LCsDeA==',
                data: userJSON,
                dataType: "json"
            }).done(function(data) {
                alert(data);
            }).fail(function(error) {
                if(error.status==401){
                    alert('Error code 401');
```

```
                              }
                              else if(error.status==400){
                                  alert('Error code 400');
                              }
                              else{
                                  alert(error);
                              }
                      });
                      event.preventDefault(); /*stop the form from
          submitting the normal way and refreshing the page*/
                 }
              });
          });
```

Now, let's understand the JavaScript code.

`$(document).ready()` binds the event of HTML page with JavaScript:

```
$("#userForm").submit(function(event){})
```

The preceding line of code captures the `submit` event of the form. Once the user fills the form and clicks on the **Submit** button, this function captures that click and runs the code written in it:

```
if($("#userId").val() && $("#username").val()){
            var id = $("#userId").val();
            var username = $("#username").val();
            var age = $("#userAge").val();
            var address = $("#userAddress").val();
            var userJSON = JSON.stringify({
                "id":id,
                "name":username,
                "age":age,
                "address":address
            });
```

In the preceding code snippet, we are checking whether the user has entered the user ID and username. After that, we create the JSON using all the details provided by the user:

```
$.ajax({
            type: "POST",
            contentType: "application/json",
    url:'https://azfntest.azurewebsites.net/api/SaveDataAPI?code=YPhjNyIo4gX2X5
    F6Nlv/6uwuKOrszcJHpRAuQeE9AzaODOA0LCsDeA==',
            data: userJSON,
            dataType: "json"
        })
```

The preceding code snippet includes some very important lines in the file. Here, we have called our API to store the data in Azure Cosmos DB. We have used **AJAX (Asynchronous JavaScript And XML)**. It is used to communicate with the servers using HTTP requests/responses. It can send and receive information in various formats, including JSON, XML, and text files.

In AJAX, first we defined the type of request: POST. After that, we specified the content type of the data we want from the server and the content type of the data we will send to the server.

Then we provided the URL parameter to AJAX that requests the API URL. This is the URL of the API, which we created at the start of the chapter using Azure Function.

With the URL, we have provided JSON data of the user and type of data.

Once the AJAX successfully calls the API and provides the data in return, it will get some response from the API and that response will come under the following section of the code:

```
done(function(data) {
        alert(data);
    })
```

It will alert the data, which will come in response.

If the API call with AJAX fails, then it will run the following code:

```
fail(function(error) {
        if(error.status==401){
            alert('Error code 401');
        }
        else if(error.status==400){
            alert('Error code 400');
        }
        else{
            alert(error);
        }
    })
```

In this, it will show the error according to the status code it gets from the API.

For example, if the status code is 401, it will simply alert that error code.

Now, right-click on the project and click on **Run**. It will open in the default browser with the URL `http://localhost:8080/SaveUserDetails/` as shown in the following screenshot:

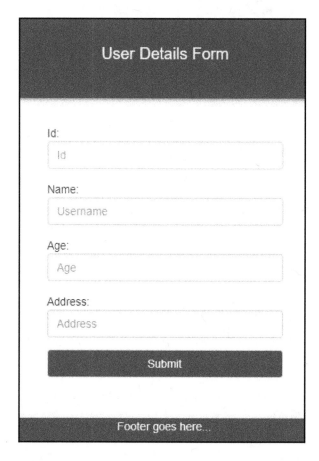

We have created a portal; now we will test it in the next section.

Using storage

We have created an API and a user form, which uses Azure Cosmos DB to store user data.

Cosmos DB is a database service that is globally distributed. It allows us to manage our data even if we keep it in datacenters that are scattered throughout the world. It provides the tools we need to scale both global distribution patterns and computational resources, and these tools are provided by Microsoft Azure.

Here are some of the advantages:

- It can support multiple data models using one backend. This means that it can be used for document, key value, relational, and graph models.
- It is more or less a NoSQL database because it does not rely on any schemas.
- It uses a query language similar to SQL and can easily support ACID transactions; some people classify it as a `NewSQL` type of database.

Test

Now, let's test our portal as follows:

1. Run the project from NetBeans. It will open the portal in the default browser.
2. Fill the form and click on the **Submit** button as shown in the following screenshot:

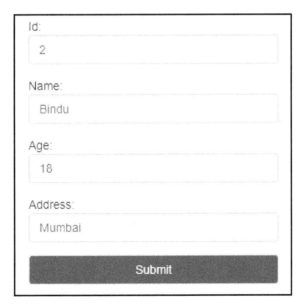

3. Once the form is processed successfully, it will give you a **Data is saved!!** popup, as shown in the following screenshot:

4. Now, to verify the entry in the database, navigate to Azure Cosmos DB, select the database, and check the entry. If the entry is there, then our portal is working fine. In our case, data is there in DB:

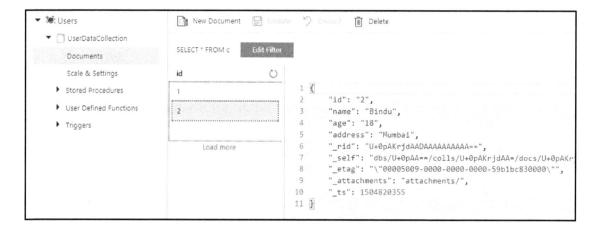

Summary

In this chapter, we learned about real-life examples of Azure Function. We have discussed the architecture of a project. We have created an API using `HttpTrigger` and Azure Cosmos DB as the output binding. We created a portal, where the user can enter their details and have it stored in Cosmos DB. After that, we discussed Cosmos DB as storage. In the last section of this chapter, we tested our portal and verified its entry in the database.

In the next chapter, we will see how to manage and deploy our code and we will learn how to configure Continuous Integration and Continuous Delivery.

7
Managing and Deploying your Code

"Do the difficult things while they are easy and do the great things while they are small. A journey of a thousand miles must begin with a single step."

– Lao Tzu

DevOps is currently one of the most discussed terms at conferences, in technical discussions, team meetings, and in customer engagements too. It is a buzzword nowadays and everyone wants to implement DevOps practices to gain the advantages of them.

Let's be very clear on the definition of DevOps. This term is a combination of development and operations. DevOps is not a tool or a technology or a framework. DevOps is a culture. It is a culture that brings improvement in the outcome and productivity of the resources.

As we have already stated, it is not a tool or technology; however, tools and technology play an important role in the implementation of DevOps practices. Along with tools, technology, and disruptive innovation in information technology, there are two other important aspects that play a major role in cultivating the DevOps culture:

- People
- Processes

The combination of people, processes, and tools therefore play a major part in this change of culture.

In this chapter, we will discuss DevOps practices, such as **Continuous Integration (CI)** and **Continuous Delivery (CD)**, using Microsoft Azure Functions and **Visual Studio Team Services (VSTS)**.

In this chapter, we will cover the following topics:

- Projects in VSTS
- Continuous Integration
- Continuous Delivery

Projects in VSTS

We want to achieve CI/CD as depicted in the following diagram:

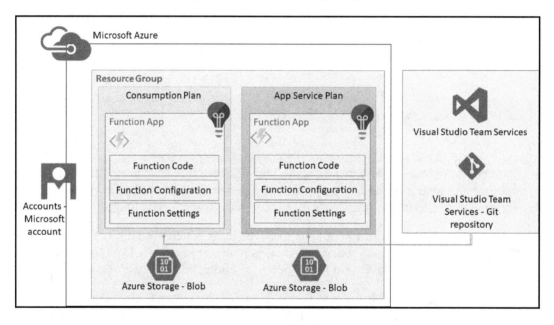

We will utilize **Visual Studio Team Services** (**VSTS**) for Continuous Integration and Continuous Delivery to deploy Azure Functions as and when code changes are committed in the Git repository hosted in VSTS:

1. First, we will create a project in VSTS so that we can store code and configure Continuous Integration and Continuous Delivery using the build and release definitions:

2. Visit `visualstudio.com` and sign in:

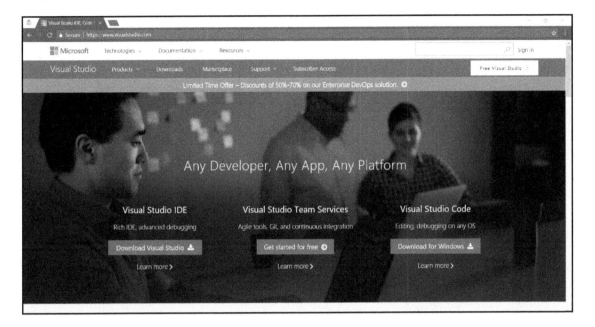

3. On the VSTS dashboard, create a new account or select an existing account.
4. We already have a few projects available in the dashboard.
5. Click on **New Project**:

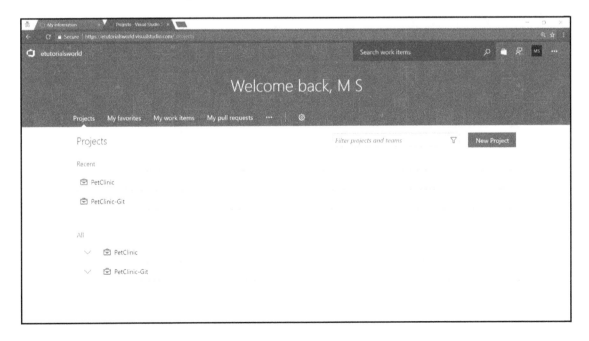

6. Provide the details for the **Project name**, **Version control**, and **Work item process**. Click on **Create**:

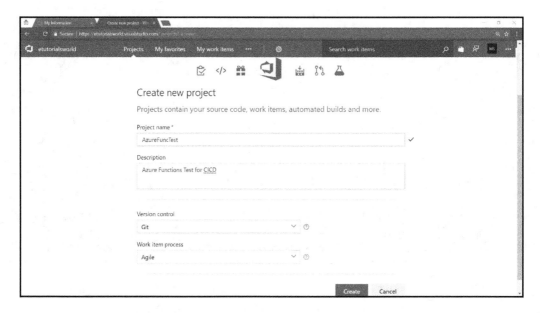

7. Click on **Generate Git credentials**:

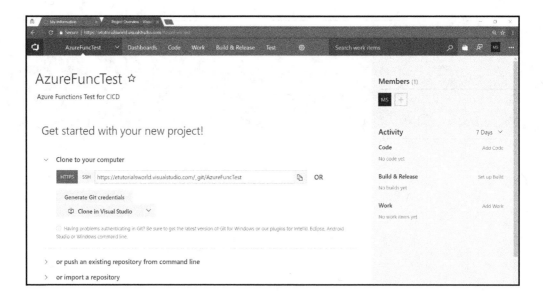

8. Provide the details as required and click on **Save Git Credentials**:

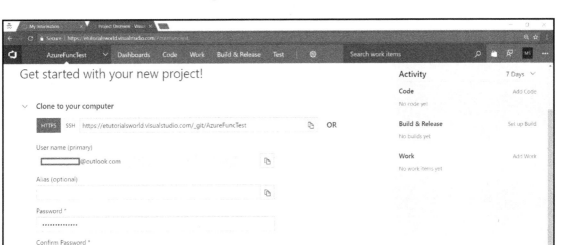

9. Once we have Git set up in the VSTS dashboard, go to the directory where Azure Function code is available.

10. If Git for Windows is not installed, then install it first.

11. Right click in the directory window and click on **Git Bash Here**:

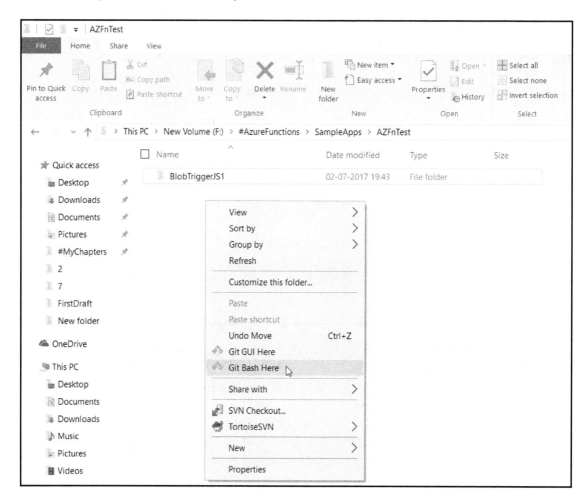

12. Initialize the Git repository with the `git init` command.
13. Verify the status of the git status command in the Git Bash.
14. Execute the `git add.` command.
15. Verify the `git status` command and now we can see that both files are tracked.

16. Execute the `git commit` command to commit the code to the local repository.

```
MINGW64 /f/#AzureFunctions/SampleApps/AZFnTest

Mitesh@LAPTOP-FQ8JSR2E MINGW64 /f/#AzureFunctions/SampleApps/AZFnTest
$ git init
Initialized empty Git repository in F:/#AzureFunctions/SampleApps/AZFnTest/.git/

Mitesh@LAPTOP-FQ8JSR2E MINGW64 /f/#AzureFunctions/SampleApps/AZFnTest (master)
$ git status
On branch master

Initial commit

Untracked files:
  (use "git add <file>..." to include in what will be committed)

        BlobTriggerJS1/

nothing added to commit but untracked files present (use "git add" to track)

Mitesh@LAPTOP-FQ8JSR2E MINGW64 /f/#AzureFunctions/SampleApps/AZFnTest (master)
$ git add .
warning: LF will be replaced by CRLF in BlobTriggerJS1/index.js.
The file will have its original line endings in your working directory.

Mitesh@LAPTOP-FQ8JSR2E MINGW64 /f/#AzureFunctions/SampleApps/AZFnTest (master)
$ git status
On branch master

Initial commit

Changes to be committed:
  (use "git rm --cached <file>..." to unstage)

        new file:   BlobTriggerJS1/function.json
        new file:   BlobTriggerJS1/index.js

Mitesh@LAPTOP-FQ8JSR2E MINGW64 /f/#AzureFunctions/SampleApps/AZFnTest (master)
```

17. From VSTS, copy the `git remote` command and execute in Git Bash.
18. Execute the `git push` command to execute the push operation on the code of Azure Functions:

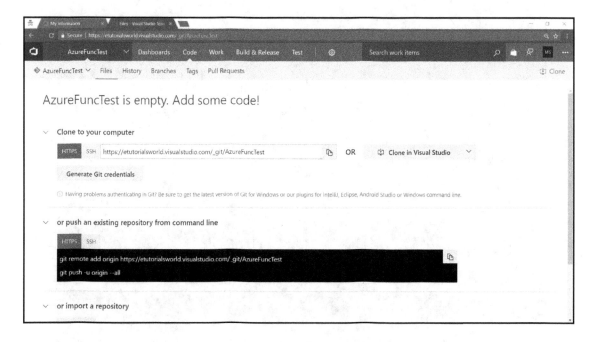

19. It will prompt for Azure sign in. Provide the username. Click on **Next**:

20. Provide the password and click on **Sign in**:

21. The code will be pushed to the Git repository configured in VSTS:

```
Mitesh@LAPTOP-FQ8JSR2E MINGW64 /f/#AzureFunctions/SampleApps/AZFnTest (master)
$ git commit -m "First Commit to VSTS"
[master (root-commit) 0718fcd] First Commit to VSTS
 2 files changed, 43 insertions(+)
 create mode 100644 BlobTriggerJS1/function.json
 create mode 100644 BlobTriggerJS1/index.js

Mitesh@LAPTOP-FQ8JSR2E MINGW64 /f/#AzureFunctions/SampleApps/AZFnTest (master)
$ git remote add origin https://etutorialsworld.visualstudio.com/_git/AzureFuncT

Mitesh@LAPTOP-FQ8JSR2E MINGW64 /f/#AzureFunctions/SampleApps/AZFnTest (master)
$ git push -u origin --all
Counting objects: 5, done.
Delta compression using up to 4 threads.
Compressing objects: 100% (4/4), done.
Writing objects: 100% (5/5), 846 bytes | 0 bytes/s, done.
Total 5 (delta 0), reused 0 (delta 0)
remote: Analyzing objects... (5/5) (7 ms)
remote: Storing packfile... done (365 ms)
remote: Storing index... done (43 ms)
To https://etutorialsworld.visualstudio.com/_git/AzureFuncTest
 * [new branch]      master -> master
Branch master set up to track remote branch master from origin.

Mitesh@LAPTOP-FQ8JSR2E MINGW64 /f/#AzureFunctions/SampleApps/AZFnTest (master)
$ |
```

22. Go to VSTS and click on the **Code** section to verify whether the code is available in the repository or not:

In the next section, we will configure Continuous Integration.

Continuous Integration

Continuous Integration is one of the most popular and core DevOps practices. Continuous Integration is a practice where code is committed to a shared repository such as Git, and the committed code is verified against static code analysis, automated build, and unit test cases.

1. Let's create a build definition.
2. Click on the Git repository and click on **Set up build**:

3. Select a template **Azure Web App** and click on **Apply**:

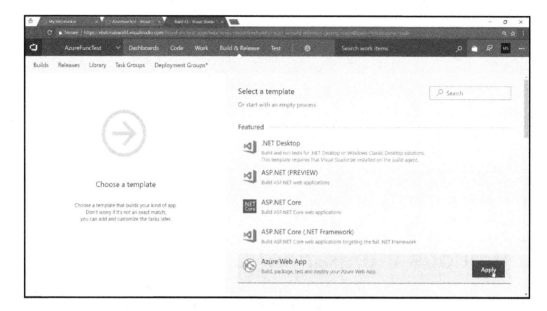

4. Keep only **Get sources** and **Publish Artifact** tasks.
5. Click on **Add Task** and add **Copy Files** task to the Build definition:

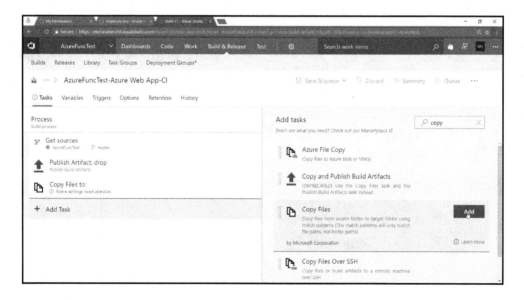

6. We want to copy all the files available from the Azure Functions project.
7. Provide the details for **Target Folder**:

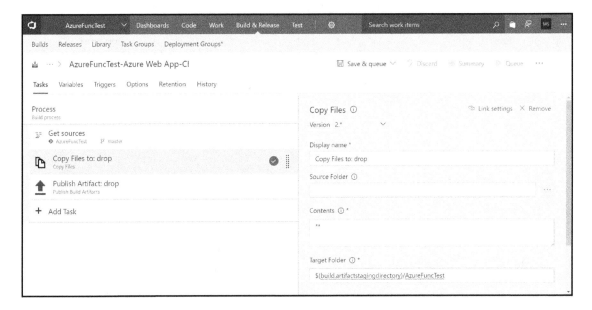

8. **Publish Artifact** is used to make available files to be used in the Release definition:

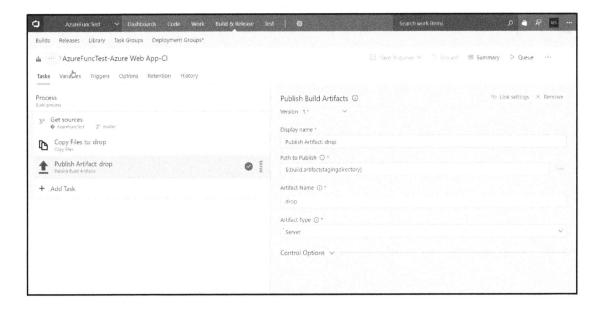

9. In the **Triggers** section, enable the Continuous Integration trigger. Now, if any new code is checked in, then Continuous Integration will take place:

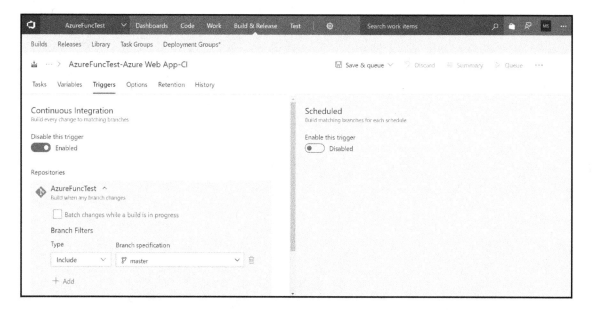

10. Click on **Save**. Our Build definition is ready.

In the next section, we will create the Release definition.

Continuous Delivery

Continuous Delivery is the practice of deploying a package into a non-production environment in an automated manner.

Once our Continuous Integration process is completed successfully, we can deploy a package using the Continuous Delivery practice in an automated way.

1. Click on the **Releases** in VSTS.

2. Click on **New definition**:

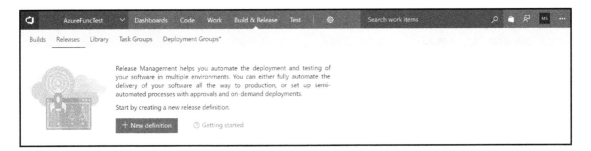

3. Select the **Azure App Service Deployment** template and click on **Next**:

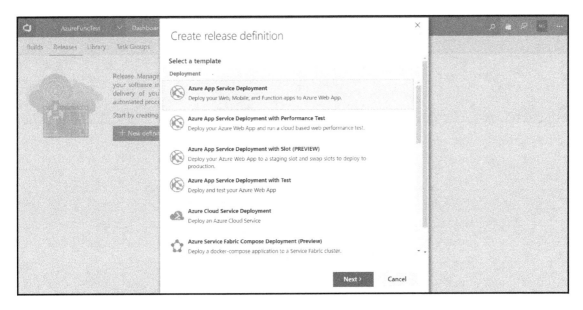

4. Select the **Project** and **Build** definition that we created in the previous section.
5. Select the Continuous Deployment checkbox.

6. It means that whenever the associated Build definition is successfully executed, release definition will be triggered automatically. Click on **Create**:

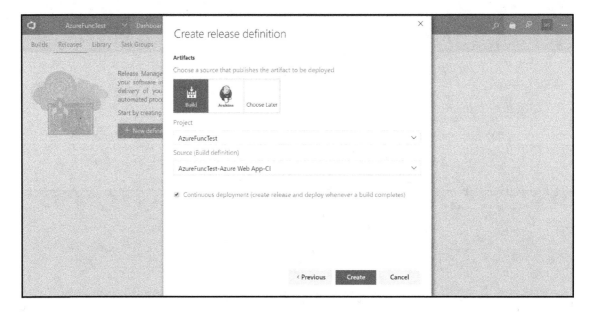

- The new Release definition is ready.
- Let's configure it.
- We need to configure Azure Subscription first.

7. Click on **Manage**:

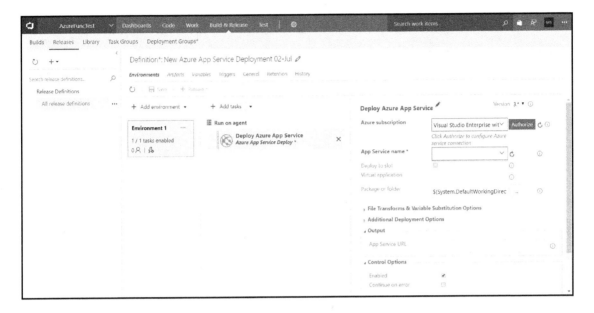

8. Click on **New Service Endpoint**.
9. Select new **Azure Resource Manager**:

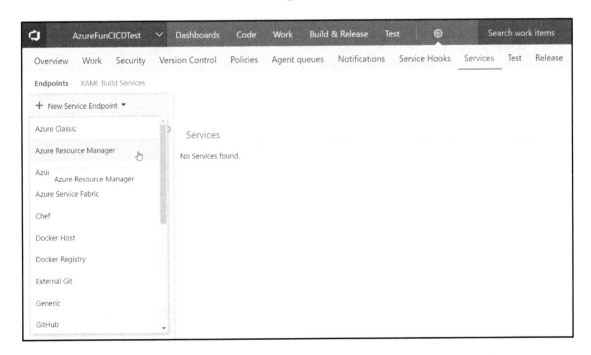

10. Provide a **Connection name** and select **Subscription**:

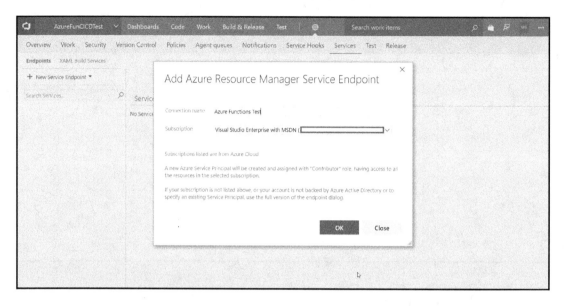

11. Verify the newly created endpoint:

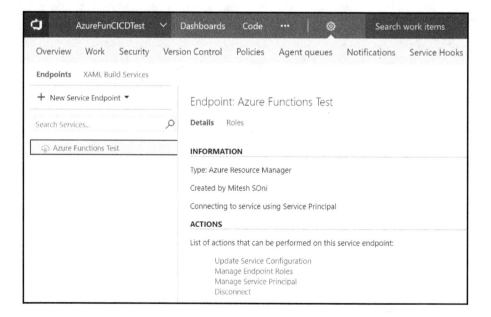

12. Go to the **Release Definitions**. Refresh the list of Azure subscriptions:

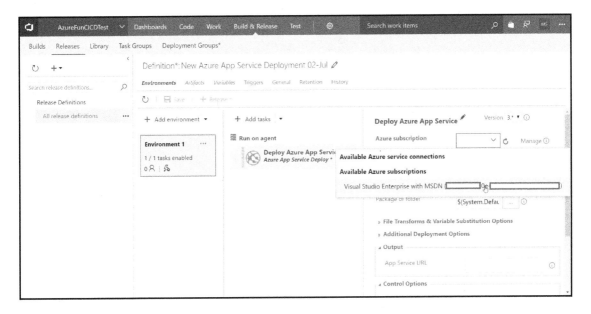

13. Click on the **Authorize** button:

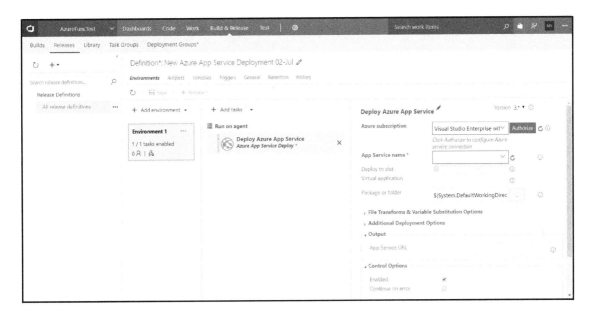

14. Refresh the list of App Service names and select the Function App created earlier.

15. Save the Release definition:

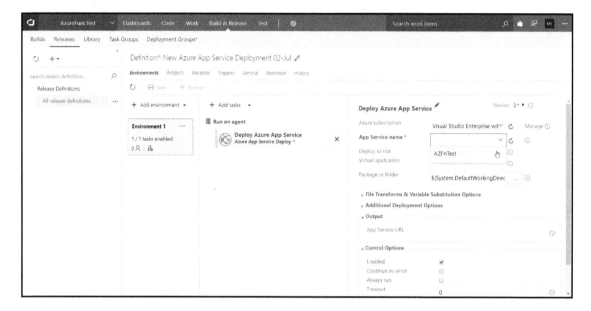

16. In the package or folder, select the location which we have given in the **Publish Artifact task** in the Build definition:

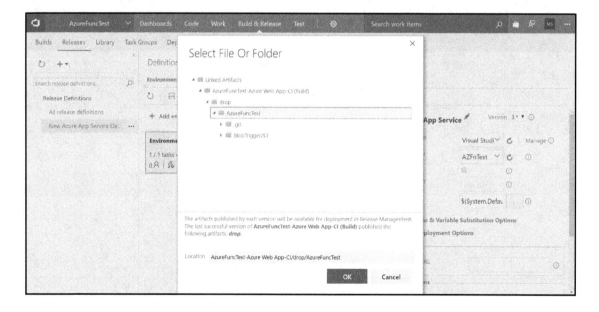

17. Now, we have the **Build & Release** definitions ready.

18. Go to the **Build** section and click on **Queue new build**.

19. Click **OK**:

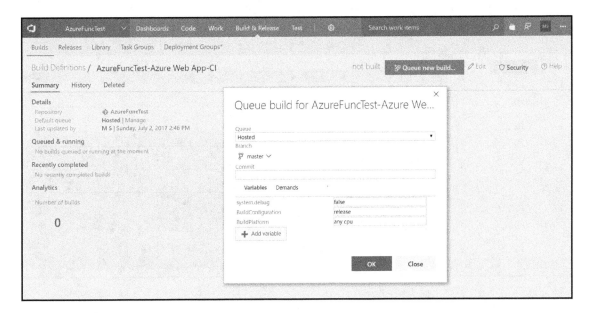

20. Wait for the availability of Hosted Agent. Hosted Agent is a virtual machine available for use where most of the required packages are available to execute the build:

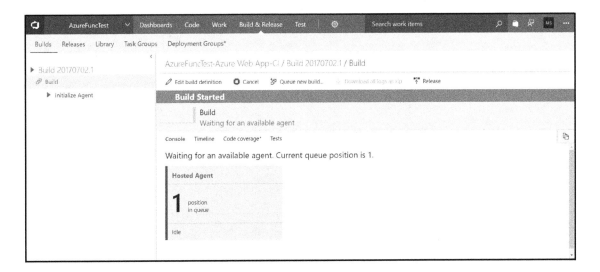

21. Once all the tasks defined in the Build definition are executed successfully, then the Build definition is successful:

22. We can click on the specific task to get the task-specific logs:

23. If in the Release definition, the trigger for Continuous Deployment is not selected, we can execute the Release definition manually too.

24. Click on **Create Release**:

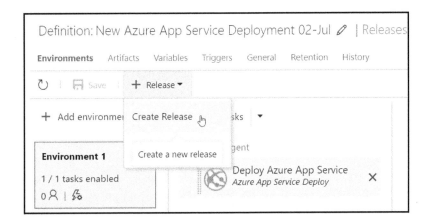

25. Select the Build version as the source and click on **Create**:

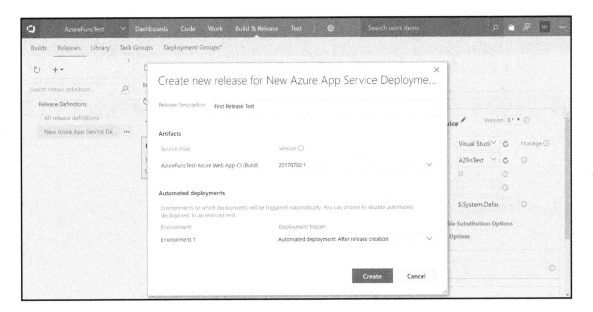

26. Observe the summary of the ongoing execution of the Release definition:

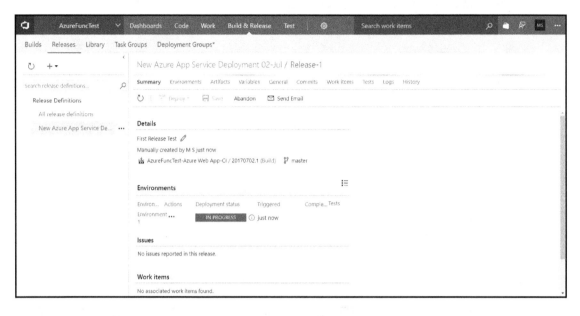

27. Click on the **Logs** tab to see the logs related to specific tasks.
28. It will download artifacts and deploy the Azure function into the Azure
    Functions app:

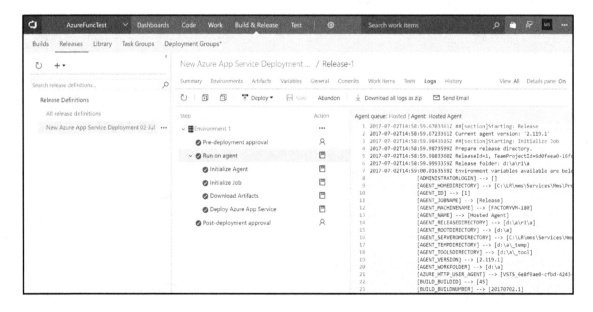

29. Verify the Function Apps in Azure Portal:

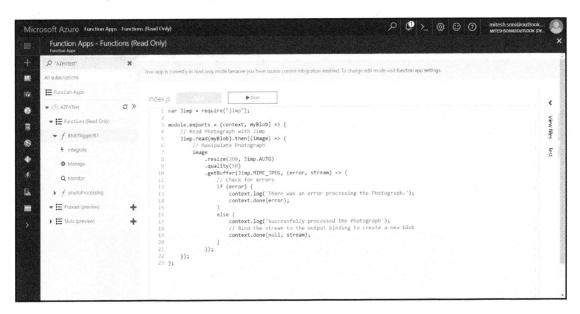

30. Go to the Kudu editor and verify the function deployment.

31. To go to the Kudu editor, and in the Azure Function URL, add `scm` after the function name:

32. Now, try to upload an image in the blob container so our function gets executed.
33. Verify whether the new function is operational or not:

34. To configure Continuous Deployment automatically, we can go to the **Triggers** tab in the Release definition:

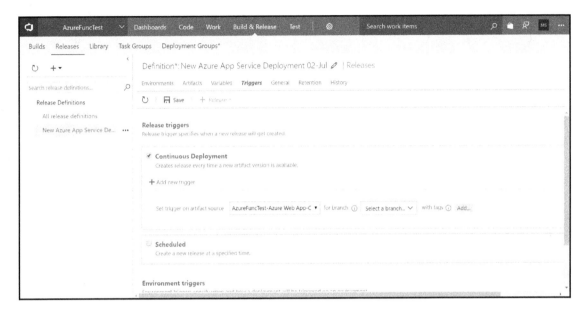

35. Now, once we have configured triggers for the Build or Release definitions; change the code:

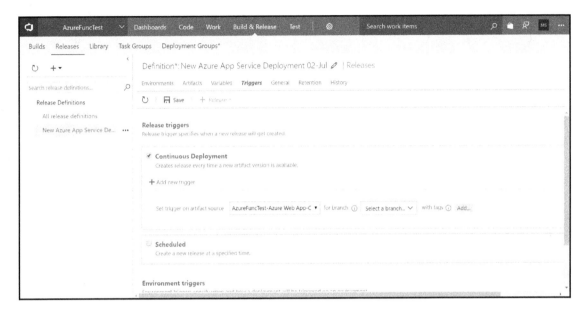

36. Verify the summary of the Build definition execution and see the **Associated Changes** section:

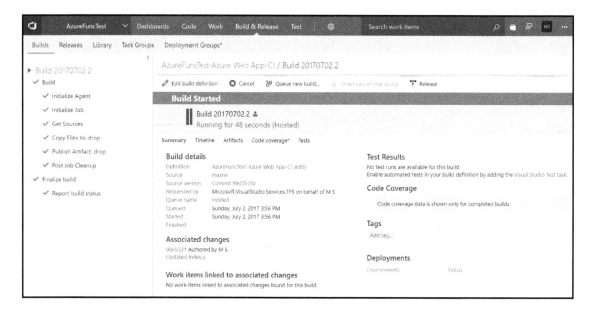

37. Once the Build execution is completed successfully, the Release definition will execute immediately.

38. Verify the Summary of the Release definition and see if it is triggered by the Build definition that we have created:

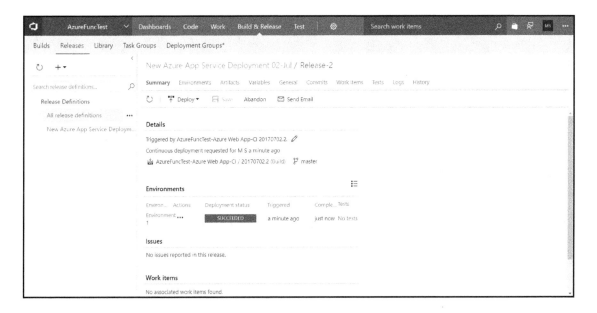

39. After the Release definition is executed successfully, upload another image in the blob container and verify the logs of the Azure Function:

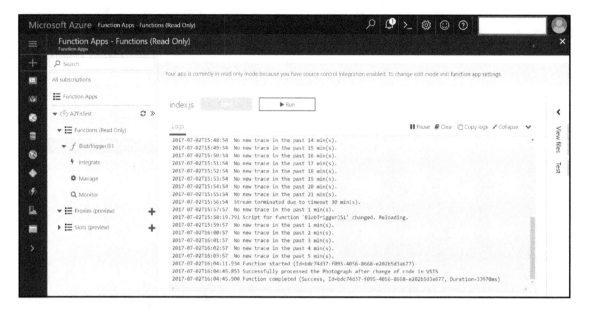

Done.

We have configured Continuous Integration and Continuous Delivery for Azure Functions.

Summary

DevOps is a culture and it is more effective when people, processes, and technology come along together to change the culture.

In serverless computing too, we can utilize DevOps practices such as Continuous Integration and Continuous Delivery.

In this chapter, we have configured Continuous Integration using the Build definition and Continuous Delivery using the Release definition. We have executed them manually and also configured the Build and Release definitions triggers.

We have also used the Git repository available in VSTS for code management.

In the next chapter, we will discuss the different options available for monitoring, pricing-related details, and best practices.

8
Business Considerations

"Do not wait; the time will never be 'just right.' Start where you stand, and work with whatever tools you may have at your command, and better tools will be found as you go along."

- George Herbert

Some considerations that most developers need to take into account when deciding to use functions as the solution are monitoring, pricing/hosting plans, and best practices.

Monitoring is one of the important aspects related to application life cycle management and we need to configure all the available configurations of monitoring in Azure.

Once we are ready with Azure Function Apps, it is very important for us to understand how to monitor the health of functions. Azure Functions have their own kind of monitoring, which are useful but basic.

For an advanced level of monitoring, we can utilize Application Insights. Another important business consideration is to understand the concepts of pricing so that we can make an informed decision based on the anticipated load, growth, and product roadmap.

In serverless computing, there have been best practices defined for the effective usage of a function as a service.

In this chapter, we will cover the following topics in detail:

- Monitoring Azure Functions
- Integration of Application Insights and Azure Functions
- Pricing/hosting plans
- Best practices

Monitoring of Azure Functions

Monitoring is essential for the quality of the Azure Functions over a specific period of time. Azure Function Apps provide a simple yet understandable monitoring in the Azure portal itself.

Go to **Function Apps**, select a specific function, and click on the **Monitor** link.

Here we can see the success count, error count, function invocation log, and other details:

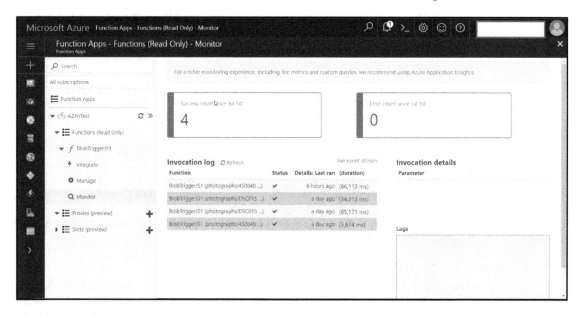

In Azure Portal, click on the function and select **Expand** to get logs in a large window, as shown in the following figure.

Upload any new image in the Azure Storage container and wait for the function to be executed successfully:

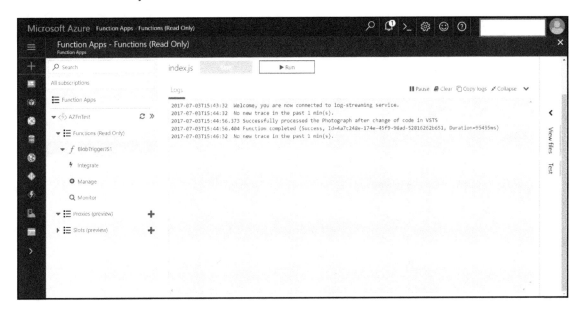

Once the function is executed successfully, go to the **Monitor** section and find the updated success count:

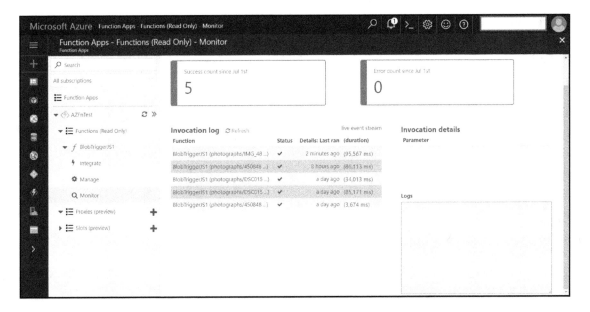

We can also set the **Daily Usage Quota** in the Azure Portal for the Function App. We can set the quota as GB per second:

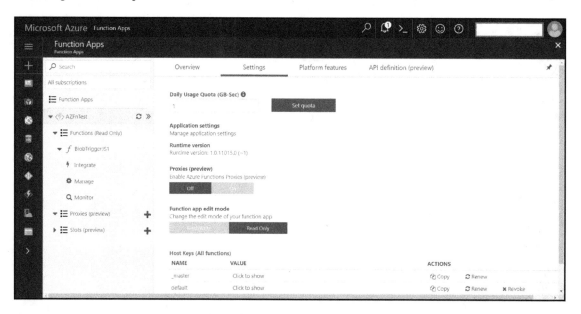

Go to the **Platform features** of the Function App and navigate to the **Properties** link to find the available properties for that specific Function App:

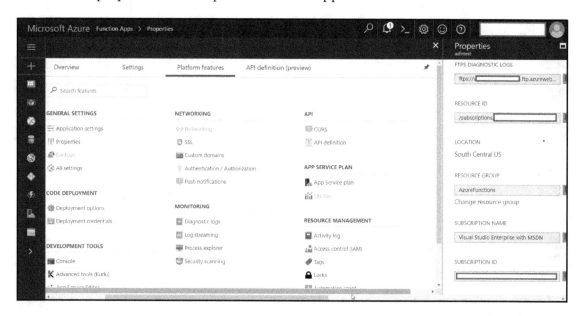

In the **Monitoring section**, click on **Diagnostic logs** and enable **Application logging, Web server logging, Detailed error messages**, and **Failed request tracing**.

Detailed error messages and **Failed request tracing** are helpful in troubleshooting.

Click on **Save**:

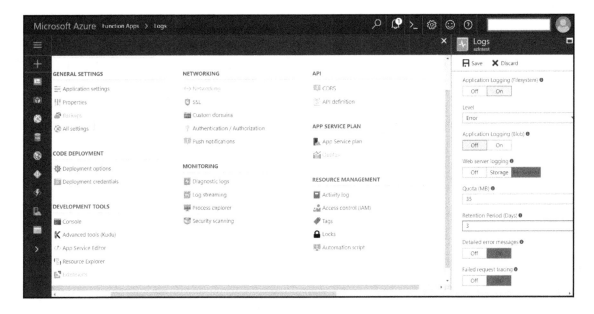

In the **Monitoring** section, click on **Log streaming** and check **Application logs** and **Web server logs**:

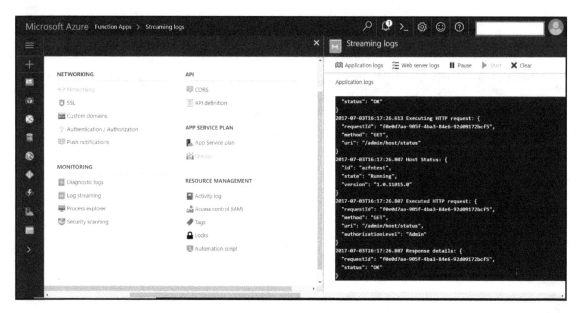

In the **Monitoring** section, **Process Explorer** provides the process ID for Kudu and the app service in Function Apps:

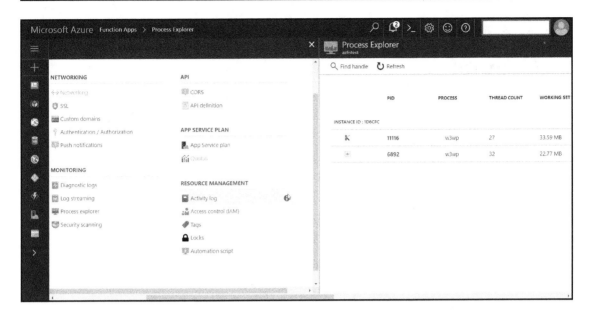

In the **Monitoring** section, security scanning with **Tinfoil Security** is available but for that we need to pay extra:

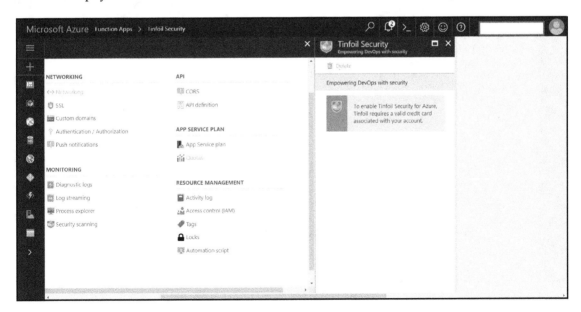

In the next section, we will discuss Application Insights for monitoring Azure Functions.

Integration of Application Insights and Azure Functions

Application Insights is used to monitor live web applications. Application Insights detects issues. It can therefore be useful in improving the quality and performance of the application. It supports applications based on .NET, Node.js, and J2EE.

Application Insights monitors request rates, dependency rates, response times, failure rates, exceptions, page views, load performance, AJAX calls, user and session counts, performance counters, host diagnostics, diagnostic trace logs, custom events, and metrics.

To integrate Azure Functions with Application Insights perform the following steps:

1. Here, we will try to use Application Insights for the Azure Function App. We have already created the Function App. Let's create Application Insights and associate it with the Function App.
2. Go to **Application Insights**.
3. Click on **Add**:

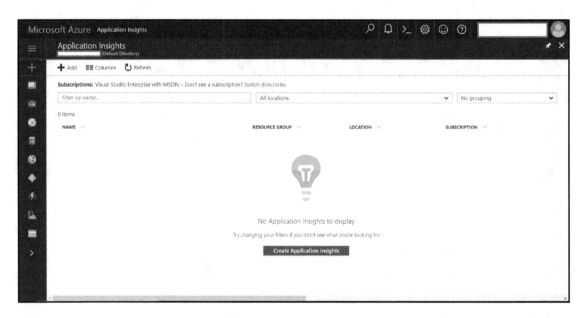

4. Give a **Name**.
5. Select **General** in **Application Type**:

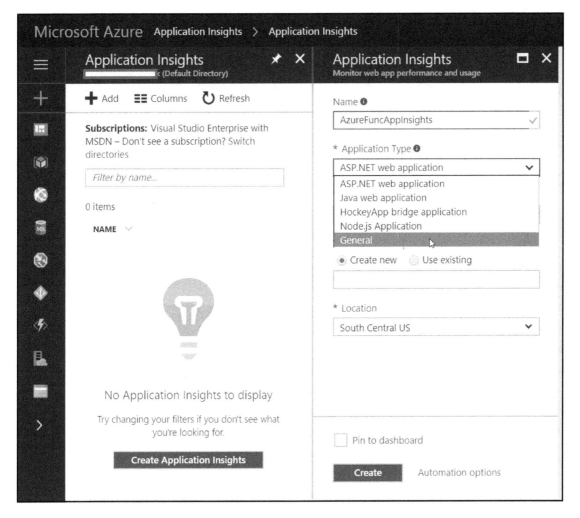

6. Use the existing **Resource Group** and select **Location**.

7. Click on **Create**:

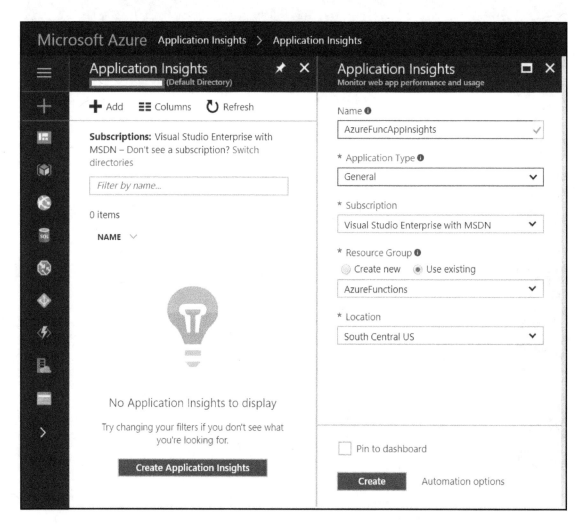

8. Once Application Insights is ready, go to the **Overview** section and note the **Instrumentation Key**:

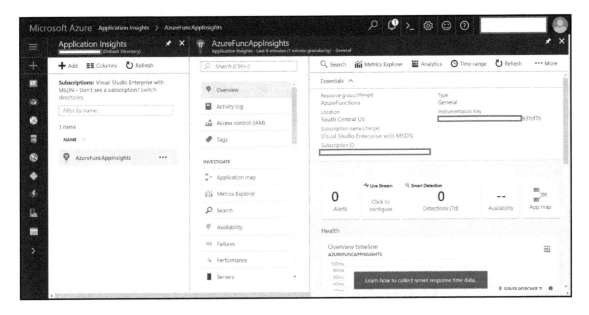

9. Go to the Function App's settings.

10. Add the **App setting** `APPINSIGHTS_INSTRUMENTATIONKEY` in **App settings** in **Application settings**:

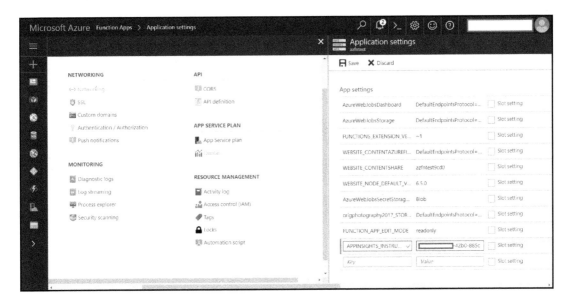

11. Once **APPINSIGHTS_INSTRUMENTATIONKEY** is configured properly, go to the instance of Application Insights and verify the **Live Metrics Stream**:

12. Go to Azure Functions and execute the function we created earlier. Once the execution is successful, go to the Application Insights instance and verify the **Live Metrics Stream**:

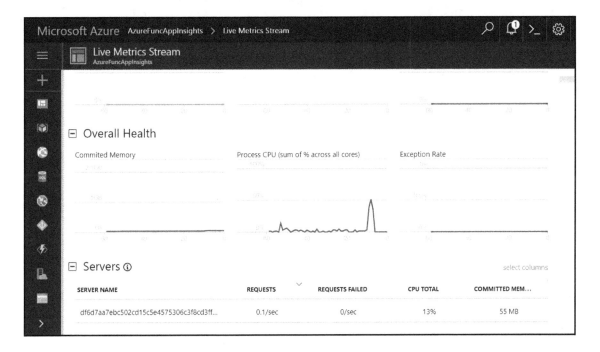

13. Click on the **Overview** section and verify the **Health** of the Azure Function App:

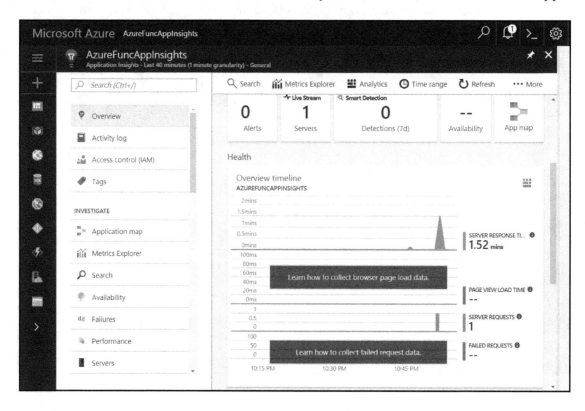

14. In the Application Insights instance, go to the **Servers** section and we can see **PROCESS CPU**, **AVAILABLE MEMORY**, and other details too:

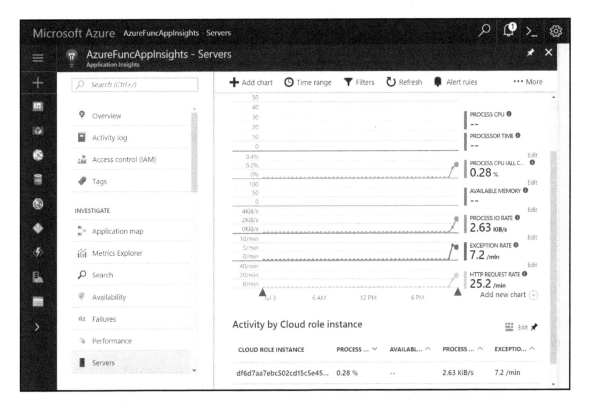

In the next section, we will discuss the pricing plan for Azure Functions.

Pricing/hosting plans

For Azure Functions, the consumption plan and App Service Plan can both be utilized:

- **Consumption plan**: In consumption plan hosting, we only pay for the time of execution of the function and not for the entire duration.

- **App Service plan**: In App Service plan hosting, we need to pay for all the resources allocated under the App Service plan for the entire time the App Service plan exists:

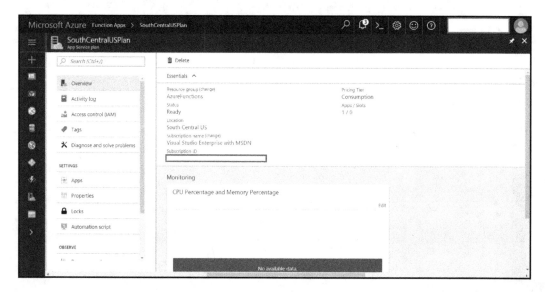

In earlier chapters, we have utilized the consumption plan for all our functions. Go to **App Services** and verify the plan:

Go to **Function Apps** in Azure Portal and verify the App Service plan; it is the same as the consumption plan:

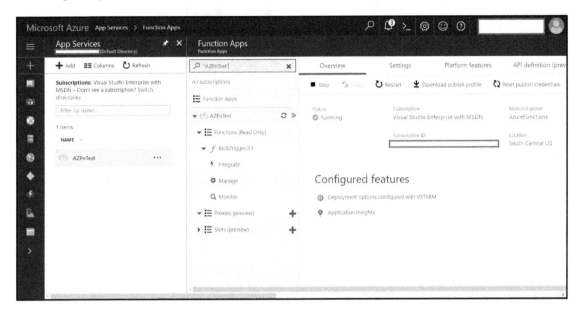

Let's see how to create Azure Functions in the App Service plan:

1. Create a new Function App.
2. In the App Service plan, click on **Create New**.
3. Provide the **App Service plan** name, **Location**, and **Pricing tier** details.

4. Click on **OK**:

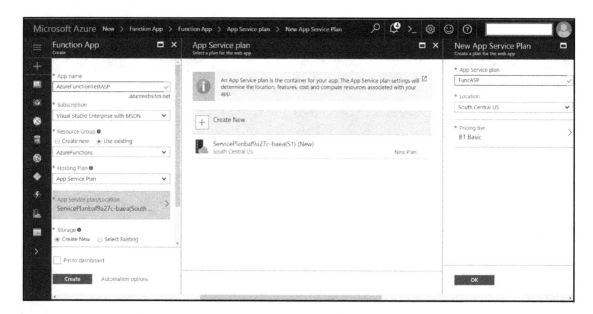

5. Click on **Create** to create the Function App in the App Service plan:

6. Now, we have two Function Apps in the Azure dashboard available. One has the consumption plan while the other has the App Service plan:

In the next section, we will list out some best practices for writing Azure Functions in order to utilize serverless architecture effectively for day-to-day usage.

Best practices

The following are recommended best practices for using Azure Functions:

- It is desirable to have stateless code to effectively utilize the serverless concept.
- Keep functions short and simple. Create many short and simple functions rather than one big function.
- Import dependencies only if they are required. Consider module dependencies as well.
- Use storage queues, service bus queues, service bus topics, and event hubs for cross-functional communication.
- Delete functions that you are no longer using, especially if the function is hosted on the App Service plan in the basic, standard, or premium tier.
- Use the built-in monitoring of Function Apps to view and optimize request latencies or utilize Application Insights.

Summary

This is the second to last chapter and we are about to finish our journey. We have covered how to monitor a Functions App using the available monitoring in the Function App itself.

Basic monitoring includes the success and error count of code execution and logs. However, it is important to have detailed analysis as well; thus, we utilized Application Insights to monitor Azure Functions.

We have integrated Azure Functions with Application Insights.

Once we decide on the usage of Azure Functions, it is important to consider pricing also, so we have also discussed the consumption plan and App Service plan to host Azure Functions.

In the next chapter, we will cover basic examples of other languages, such as Python, PHP, and so on.

9
Working with Different Languages

"Elegance is not a dispensable luxury but a factor that decides between success and failure"

– Edsger Dijkstra

In this chapter, we will explore Azure Function with other languages. Up to now we have seen examples of Azure Function in JavaScript.

We can write Azure Functions in many languages such as C#, Python, F#, PHP, and JavaScript.

In this chapter, we will write Azure Functions in the following languages:

- The Python Function App
- The PHP Function App

Python as an *object-based* subset is roughly equivalent to JavaScript. Like JavaScript, Python supports a programming style that uses simple functions and variables without engaging in class definitions. Python, on the other hand, supports writing much larger programs and better code reuse through a true object-oriented programming style, where classes and inheritance play an important role. Python has built-in list and dictionary data structures, which can be used to construct fast runtime data structures.

PHP is open source. It is a server-side scripting language. PHP has both procedure programming language and OOP language features. It uses C-like syntax, so for those who are familiar with C, it's very easy for them to pick up and create website scripts. It is relatively faster since it mostly uses system resources.

The Python Function App

Let's create a Python Function in Azure App. We already created Azure App in the previous chapter.

Python is still in the experimental phase, so we don't have much of an option as of now.

Now, we will create a Python Function and learn how to install and use third-party modules.

Example

We will create an HTTP request API which gives a weather report in JSON format in response. In this example, we will use Google Weather API, which is open source:

1. Log into the Azure Portal and create Azure App. We have created Azure App in the previous chapter. Now we will create the function. Click on the + sign and select the language, as shown in the following screenshot:

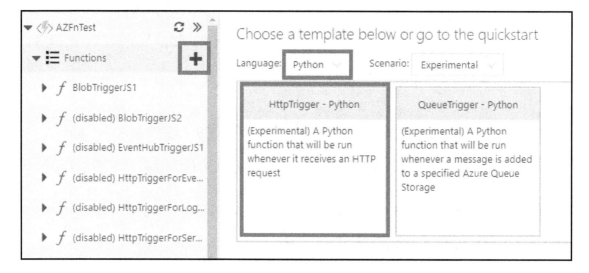

2. There are only two options available for us, that is **HttpTrigger - Python** and **QueueTrigger - Python**:
   - **HttpTrigger - Python**: This trigger gets fired whenever it receives an Http request
   - **QueueTrigger - Python**: This trigger gets fired when a message is added to specified Azure Queue storage

3. Select **HttpTrigger - Python**. Now, we will provide a name for the function and click on the **Create** button:

4. It will create a default `Hello world!` template for us, as shown in the following screenshot:

```python
run.py    Save    ▶ Run

1 import os
2 import json
3
4 postreqdata = json.loads(open(os.environ['req']).read())
5 response = open(os.environ['res'], 'w')
6 response.write("hello world from "+postreqdata['name'])
7 response.close()
```

5. Now, we will install the `pprint` module for this function. This module is used to print JSON on the console. To use pprint, we need to install this package. Once we have installed it, we can use this module in our Azure Function:

- To install the module for the function, click on Azure Function **Overview** and get the **URL**:

- Navigate to Kudu Console using `URL:Consider` this example:

   https://Your_APP_NAME.scm.azurewebsites.net/DebugConsole

- On the console, navigate to `D:\home\site\tools` and write the following command:

   python.exe -m pip install pprint -user

   The output is shown in the following screenshot:

```
PS D:\home\site\tools> python.exe -m pip install pprint --user
Downloading/unpacking pprint
  Downloading pprint-0.1.tar.gz
  Running setup.py (path:d:\local\temp\pip_build_RD000D3A7110AD$\pprint\setup.py) egg_info for package pprint

Installing collected packages: pprint
  Running setup.py install for pprint

Successfully installed pprint
Cleaning up...
PS D:\home\site\tools>
```

- Now, our `pprint` module is installed and we are ready to use the module in our code.

- The `pprint` module provides a capability to "pretty-print" arbitrary Python data structures in a form which can be used as input to the interpreter. It prints the formatted representation of the object on the stream, followed by a newline.
- It formats our object and writes it to the data stream passed as argument.

6. Modify the default code as shown in the following screenshot:

```python
import os
import urllib2
import json
from pprint import pprint

#request parameter
postreqdata = json.loads(open(os.environ['req']).read())

latlong = postreqdata['latlong']

#google weather API Opensource
url = "https://api.forecast.io/forecast/1c063ba01a246881d41eb22345b7e1bf/"+latlong+"?units=si"

data = json.load(urllib2.urlopen(url))

#Pre-define function demo
print len(data), "weather"

#loop demo
for obj in data:
    print obj

#install moduledemo
pprint(data)

#set response
response = open(os.environ['res'], 'w')
response.write(json.dumps(data))
response.close()
```

7. Save and run the preceding code with the `latlong` as request parameter, as shown in the following screenshot:

8. You can see the output of this request in **Response body**. We can try this by providing the latitude and longitude of different cities.

9. Now, let's understand the code:

- The module we installed will be imported to the code, as shown in the following screenshot:

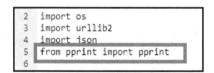

- Use of `pprint` is shown in the following screenshot. We have used this only to print JSON in the console. This is just for a demo of adding external modules and using Python code:

```
24  #install module demo
25  pprint(data)
26
```

10. Now that our API is created, we can use it. Get the URL for the API, as shown in the following screenshot:

11. Click on **</>Get function URL** once—we will see a pop-up, and copy the URL from there:

12. Now we can use the Chrome extension Postman to test our API. Paste the API URL in Postman and provide the request body and check the response.

13. Refer to the following screenshot:

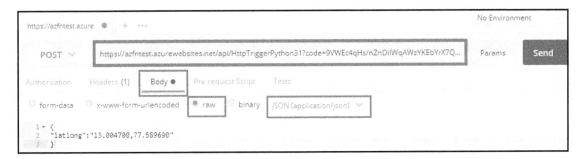

14. After providing all the parameters, click on the **Send** button. Now, scroll down and check the response, as shown in the following screenshot:

```
Body     Cookies     Headers (11)     Tests

Pretty    Raw     Preview     JSON  ∨    ⇥

1 ▾  {
2 ▾      "hourly": {
3            "icon": "rain",
4 ▾          "data": [
5 ▾              {
6                    "ozone": 264.19,
7                    "windGust": 11.02,
8                    "temperature": 23.07,
9                    "icon": "rain",
10                   "precipType": "rain",
11                   "humidity": 0.83,
12                   "cloudCover": 0.58,
13                   "summary": "Light Rain",
14                   "apparentTemperature": 23.59,
15                   "pressure": 1003.83,
16                   "windSpeed": 7.36,
17                   "time": 1503221400,
18                   "windBearing": 263,
19                   "precipIntensity": 1.2395,
20                   "uvIndex": 5,
21                   "dewPoint": 19.93,
22                   "precipProbability": 0.42
23               },
```

15. Now we have created the Python example.

The PHP Function App

Let's create a PHP Function in Azure App. We already created Azure App in the previous chapter.

PHP is also still in the experimental phase, so we don't have much of an option as of now.

Example

Now we will create an Azure Function with the DNS lookup example in PHP:

1. Log into Azure Portal and click on **Azure Function App**. We already created Azure Function App in the previous chapter, so now we will create the Azure Function.

2. Click on the + sign and then select the coding language, as shown in the following screenshot:

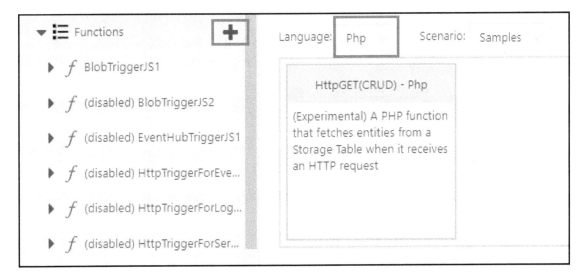

By default, PHP gives the template that fetches the entities from a storage table when it receives the HTTP request.

The code for fetching a data from the storage table is already there in PHP. We can directly use it. However, in this example, we will not use the storage table. We will write code for DNS lookup.

This allows us to create only the HTTP GET request:

1. Now, give a name to the function, provide the storage account connection, and click on the **Create** button.

2. Even if we are not using the storage connection, we still need to provide a storage account connection because until now we don't have much of an option for PHP. PHP code is in experimental mode, so in the future this will not be the case:

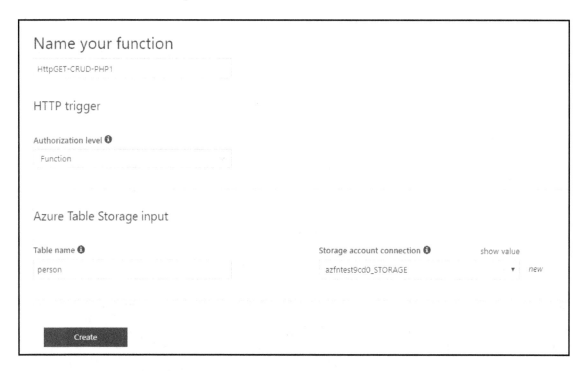

3. By default, it will give the following template:

```php
<?php
$inTable = json_decode(file_get_contents(getenv('inTable')));
file_put_contents(getenv('res'), json_encode($inTable));
?>
```

We can directly write this code. Add some entity in the storage table and run this code. We will get all the entity stored in the storage table. This is the HTTP get request, so we use the function URL and hit that URL in the browser to check the response:

1. Now we will modify the code, as shown in the following screenshot:

```
run.php       Save              ▶ Run

1  <?php
2  $ip = gethostbyname("www.google.com");
3  echo "IP = $ip\n";
4  $host = gethostbyaddr("192.0.34.166");
5  echo "Host = $host\n";
6  $ip = gethostbynamel("yahoo.com");
7  print_r($ip);
8  file_put_contents(getenv('res'), json_encode($ip));
9  ?>
```

2. Let's understand the code first, then we will run and test the HTTP APIs:

```
2  <?php
3
4  $ip = gethostbyname("www.google.com");
5  echo "IP = $ip\n";
6
```

3. In the preceding code, `gethostbyname()` is a predefined function in PHP, which takes the name of the host and returns its IP address. `gethostbyaddr()` is also a predefined function, which takes the IP address as input and returns the name of the host:

```
6
7  $host = gethostbyaddr("192.0.34.166");
8  echo "Host = $host\n";
9
```

4. The next line of the code prints the array response, as shown in the following screenshot:

```
11
12  print_r($ip);
13
```

5. Finally, the response is set for the HTTP request:

```
13
14 file_put_contents(getenv('res'), json_encode($ip));
15 ?>
```

6. Now, we will test our HTTP request API. For that, get the function URL first. Click on **</> Get function URL**, as shown in the following screenshot:

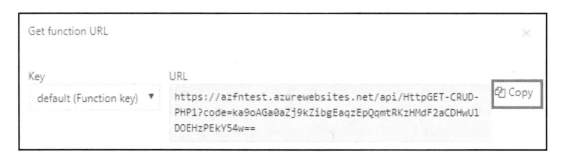

7. Once we click on **</> Get function URL**, we will see a pop-up with the URL. Click on the **Copy** button to copy the URL:

Get function URL   ✕

Key   URL

default (Function key) ▼   https://azfntest.azurewebsites.net/api/HttpGET-CRUD-   📋 Copy
                           PHP1?code=ka9oAGa0aZj9kZibgEaqzEpQqmtRKzHMdF2aCDHwU1
                           DOEHzPEkY54w==

8. Now, open any browser to check out the API. We will use Chrome to check our API, as shown in the following screenshot:

← → C 🔒 Secure | https://azfntest.azurewebsites.net/api/Http...

["98.139.180.149","98.138.253.109","206.190.36.45"]

9. Now we have created the PHP Azure Function. We can try with a different hostname and IP address.

10. Since we don't have much of an option available in Azure Function, this is a simple example to start with PHP Azure Function.

11. Try to explore more with this example by taking the parameter from the query string and then providing the response accordingly.

12. Since it is in experimental mode, it only provides us the HTTP GET request. **Request body** won't work here because currently it doesn't allow the POST request.

Summary

This is the last chapter and we have finished our journey with Azure Functions.

We started our journey with a discussion of serverless architecture with the evolution of cloud computing and we discussed in detail IaaS and PaaS.

After that we discussed Azure Functions and looked at the differences between Web App AWS Lambda and Azure Functions. We created our first function that processed a photograph and created a thumbnail. We discussed the architecture of a trigger and different types of triggers available in Azure.

In the middle of our journey, we learned about binding with the Azure Function and Webhook. After that we created a real-life example of an Azure Function and we configured Continuous Integration using the Build definition and Continuous Delivery using the Release definition.

At the end of our journey, we covered how to monitor a Functions App using the available monitoring in the Function App itself.

In this chapter we looked at other languages for writing code in Azure Function. We briefly introduced the Python and PHP Azure Function. We created the Azure Function in Python and installed the third-party module using Kudu editor. We also learned how to use that module in Python code. We created a Python HTTP API and tested it. In the following section of this chapter we created a PHP Azure Function and got some idea of PHP code and ran that code.

Index

A

App Insights 37
App Service plan (ASP) 32
App Services
  about 30
  App Service plan (ASP) 32
Application Insights
  integrating 194, 196, 198, 199, 200, 201
Asynchronous JavaScript And XML (AJAX) 153
AWS Lambda
  versus Azure Services 38
  versus AzureFunctions 38
Azure Active Directory (Azure AD) 35
Azure Functions
  about 17, 194, 196, 198, 199, 200, 201
  anatomy 42
  App Service plan 18
  best practices 205
  consumption plan 18
  event, used 126
  executing 69
  function App 42
  function code 42
  function configuration 44
  function settings 44
  monitoring 188, 189, 190
  reference link 25
  runtime 45
  setting up 45
  troubleshooting 63
  versus AWS Lambda 38
  versus Azure Services 38
  Webhook, used 123
Azure Services
  versus AWS Lambda 38
  versus AzureFunctions 38

B

bindings
  input 94
  input bindings, types 94
  No-SQL DB 94
  output 94
  output bindings, types 95
  SQL tables 94
  storage tables 94

C

Cascading Style Sheet (CSS) 151
cloud computing
  about 12
  basics 12
cloud service models
  about 14
  Infrastructure as a Service (IaaS) 13
  Platform as a Service (PaaS) 13
  Software as a Service (SaaS) 13
Continuous Delivery 170, 171, 172, 173, 174,
    175, 176, 178, 179, 180, 181, 182, 183, 184,
    185, 186
Continuous Integration 167, 168, 169, 170

E

Event Hubs
  about 90, 96
  example 96
  Service Bus 103
  types 96
event
  Blob Trigger 127
  EventHub Trigger 127
  Generic Webhook Trigger 127
  GitHub Webhook Trigger 127

HTTP Trigger 127
Queue Trigger 127
ServiceBus Queue Trigger 127
Timer Trigger 127
used, with Azure Functions 126
events
ServiceBus Topic Trigger 127

F

Function as a Service (FaaS) 16

H

HTTP trigger 81, 82, 83, 84, 85, 86, 87, 88, 89
Hyper Text Markup Language (HTML) 147

I

Infrastructure as a Service (IaaS) 13
input bindings
blob storage 94
types 94
Internet of Things (IoT) 75

J

JavaScript function
creating, triggered by Webhook 114

M

Microsoft Azure Services
App Insights 37
App Services 30
Azure Active Directory 35
overview 24
regions 24
resource groups 26
Microsoft Azure
URL 27

O

output bindings
blob storage 95
events 95
HTTP (REST or Webhook) 95
No-SQL DB 95
push notifications 95

queues and topics 95
SendGrid email 96
SQL tables 95
storage tables 95
types 95

P

PHP Function App
about 214
example 215
portal
testing 155, 156
pricing/hosting plans
about 201, 203, 204, 205
App Service plan 202
consumption plan 201
project
building 131, 132, 133, 134, 135, 136, 137,
138, 139, 140, 141, 142, 143, 144, 145, 147,
148, 149, 153, 154
outlining 129, 130
Python Function App
about 208
example 208

S

scheduled trigger
creating 75, 77, 78, 79, 80, 81
serverless architectures
cloud computing 11
overview 10
serverless computing 16
service models 11
serverless computing
about 16
benefits 16
service bus
about 91, 92
ServiceBus Queue Trigger 92
ServiceBus Topic Trigger 92
service level agreements (SLAs) 14
solution
architecting 130, 131
storage
about 108

example 109
using 154, 155

T

triggers
  BlobTrigger 75
  EventHubTrigger 75
  Generic Webhook 75
  GitHub Webhook 75
  HTTPTrigger 75
  QueueTrigger 75
  Service Bus trigger 75

TimerTrigger 75
types 74

V

Visual Studio Team Services (VSTS)
  about 158
  projects 158

W

Webhook
  JavaScript function, creating 114
  used, with Azure Functions 123